The Boys' Life

by Helen Nicolay

I. A PRESIDENT'S CHILDHOOD

Abraham Lincoln's forefathers were pioneers--men who left their homes to open up the wilderness and make the way plain for others to follow them. For one hundred and seventy years, ever since the first American Lincoln came from England to Massachusetts in 1638, they had been moving slowly westward as new settlements were made in the forest. They faced solitude, privation, and all the dangers and hardships that beset men who take up their homes where only beasts and wild men have had homes before; but they continued to press steadily forward, though they lost fortune and sometimes even life itself, in their westward progress. Back in Pennsylvania and New Jersey some of the Lincolns had been men of wealth and influence. In Kentucky, where the future President was born on February 12, 1809, his parents lived in deep poverty Their home was a small log cabin of the rudest kind, and nothing seemed more unlikely than that their child, coming into the world in such humble surroundings, was destined to be the greatest man of his time. True to his race, he also was to be a pioneer--not indeed, like his ancestors, a leader into new woods and unexplored fields, but a pioneer of a nobler and grander sort, directing the thoughts of men ever toward the right, and leading the American people, through difficulties and dangers and a mighty war, to peace and freedom.

The story of this wonderful man begins and ends with a tragedy, for his grandfather, also named Abraham, was killed by a shot from an Indian's rifle while peaceably at work with his three sons on the edge of their frontier clearing. Eighty-one years later the President himself met death by an assassin's bullet. The murderer of one was a savage of the forest; the murderer of the other that far more cruel thing, a savage of civilization.

When the Indian's shot laid the pioneer farmer low, his second son, Josiah, ran to a neighboring fort for help, and Mordecai, the eldest, hurried to the cabin for his rifle. Thomas, a child of six years, was left alone beside the dead body of his father; and as Mordecai snatched the gun from its resting-place over the door of the cabin, he saw, to his horror, an Indian in his war-paint, just stooping to seize the child. Taking quick aim at a medal on the breast of the savage, he fired, and the Indian fell dead. The little boy, thus released, ran to the house, where Mordecai, firing through the loopholes, kept the Indians at bay until help arrived from the fort.

It was this child Thomas who grew up to be the father of President Abraham Lincoln. After the murder of his father the fortunes of the little family grew rapidly worse, and doubtless because of poverty, as well as by reason of the marriage of his older brothers and sisters, their home was broken up, and Thomas found himself, long before he was grown, a wandering laboring boy. He lived for a time with an uncle as his hired servant, and later he learned the trade of carpenter. He grew to manhood entirely without education, and when he was twenty-eight years old could neither read nor write. At that time he married Nancy Hanks, a good-looking young woman of twenty-three, as poor as himself, but so much better off as to learning that she was able to teach her husband to sign his own name. Neither of them had any money, but living cost little on the frontier in those days, and they felt that his trade would suffice to earn all that they should need. Thomas took his bride to a tiny house in Elizabethtown, Kentucky, where they lived for about a year, and where a daughter was born to them.

Then they moved to a small farm thirteen miles from Elizabethtown, which they bought on credit, the country being yet so new that there were places to be had for mere promises to pay. Farms obtained on such terms were usually of very poor quality, and this one of Thomas Lincoln's was no exception to the rule. A cabin ready to be occupied stood on it, however; and not far away, hidden in a pretty clump of trees and bushes, was a fine spring of water, because of which the place was known as Rock Spring Farm. In the cabin on this farm the future President of the United States was born on February 12, 1809, and here the first four years of his life were spent. Then the Lincolns moved to a much bigger and better farm on Knob Creek, six miles from Hodgensville, which Thomas Lincoln bought, again on credit, selling the larger part of it soon afterward to another purchaser. Here they remained until Abraham was seven years old.

About this early part of his childhood almost nothing is known. He never talked of these days, even to his most intimate friends. To the pioneer child a farm offered much that a town lot could not give him--space; woods to roam in; Knob Creek with its running water and its deep, quiet pools for a playfellow; berries to be hunted for in summer and nuts in autumn; while all the year round birds and small animals pattered across his path to people the solitude in place of human companions. The boy had few comrades. He wandered about playing his lonesome little games, and when these were finished returned to the small and cheerless cabin. Once, when asked what he remembered about the War of 1812 with Great Britain, he replied: "Only this: I had been fishing one day and had caught a little fish, which I was taking home. I met a soldier in the road, and having always been told at home that we must be good to soldiers, I gave him my fish." It is only a glimpse into his life, but it shows the solitary, generous child and the patriotic household.

It was while living on this farm that Abraham and his sister Sarah first began going to A-B-C schools. Their earliest teacher was Zachariah Riney, who taught near the Lincoln cabin; the next was Caleb Hazel, four miles away.

In spite of the tragedy that darkened his childhood, Thomas Lincoln seems to have been a cheery, indolent, good-natured man. By means of a little farming and occasional jobs at his trade, he managed to supply his family with the absolutely necessary food and shelter, but he never got on in the world. He found it much easier to gossip with his friends, or to dream about rich new lands in the West, than to make a thrifty living in the place where he happened to be. The blood of the pioneer was in his veins too--the desire to move westward; and hearing glowing accounts of the new territory of Indiana, he resolved to go and see it for himself. His skill as a carpenter made this not only possible but reasonably cheap, and in the fall of 1816 he built himself a little flatboat, launched it half a mile from his cabin, at the mouth of Knob Creek on the waters of the Rolling Fork, and floated on it down that stream to Salt River, down Salt River to the Ohio, and down the Ohio to a landing called Thompson's Ferry on the Indiana shore.

Sixteen miles out from the river, near a small stream known as Pigeon Creek, he found a spot in the forest that suited him; and as his boat could not be made to float up-stream, he sold it, stored his goods with an obliging settler, and trudged back to Kentucky, all the way on foot, to fetch his wife and children-- Sarah, who was now nine years old, and Abraham, seven. This time the journey to Indiana was made with two horses, used by the mother and children for riding, and to carry their little camping outfit for the night. The distance from their old home was, in a straight line, little more than fifty miles, but they had to go double that distance because of the very few roads it was possible to follow.

Reaching the Ohio River and crossing to the Indiana shore, Thomas Lincoln hired a wagon which carried his family and their belongings the remaining sixteen miles through the forest to the spot he had chosen--a piece of heavily wooded land, one and a half miles east of what has since become the village of Gentryville in Spencer County. The lateness of the autumn made it necessary to put up a shelter as quickly as possible, and he built what was known on the frontier as a half-faced camp, about fourteen feet square. This differed from a cabin in that it was closed on only three sides, being quite open to the weather on the fourth. A fire was usually made in front of the open side, and thus the necessity for having a chimney was done away with. Thomas Lincoln doubtless intended this only for a temporary shelter, and as such it would have done well enough in pleasant summer weather; but it was a rude provision against the storms and winds of an Indiana winter. It shows his want of energy that the family remained housed in this poor camp for nearly a whole year; but, after all, he must not be too hastily blamed. He was far from idle. A cabin was doubtless begun, and there was the very heavy work of clearing away the timber--cutting down large trees, chopping them into suitable lengths, and rolling them together into great heaps to be burned, or of splitting them into rails to fence the small field upon which he managed to raise a patch of corn and other things during the following summer.

Though only seven years old, Abraham was unusually large and strong for his age, and he helped his father in all this heavy labor of clearing the farm. In after years, Mr. Lincoln said that an ax "was put into his hands at once, and from that till within his twenty-third year he was almost constantly handling that most useful instrument--less, of course, in ploughing and harvesting seasons." At first the Lincolns and their seven or eight neighbors lived in the unbroken forest. They had only the tools and household goods they brought with them, or such things as they could fashion with their own hands. There was no sawmill to saw lumber. The village of Gentryville was not even begun. Breadstuff could be had only by sending young Abraham seven miles on horseback with a bag of corn to be ground in a hand grist-mill.

About the time the new cabin was ready relatives and friends followed from Kentucky, and some of these in turn occupied the half-faced camp. During the autumn a severe and mysterious sickness broke out in their little settlement, and a number of people died, among them the mother of young Abraham. There was no help to be had beyond what the neighbors could give each other. The nearest doctor lived fully thirty miles away. There was not even a minister to conduct the funerals. Thomas Lincoln made the coffins for the dead out of green lumber cut from the forest trees with a whip-saw, and they were laid to rest in a clearing in the woods. Months afterward, largely through the efforts of the sorrowing boy, a preacher who chanced to come that way was induced to hold a service and preach a sermon over the grave of Mrs. Lincoln.

Her death was indeed a serious blow to her husband and children. Abraham's sister, Sarah, was only eleven years old, and the tasks and cares of the little household were altogether too heavy for her years and experience. Nevertheless they struggled bravely through the winter and following summer; then in the autumn of 1819 Thomas Lincoln went back to Kentucky and married Sarah Bush Johnston, whom he had known, and it is said courted, when she was only Sally Bush. She had married about the time Lincoln married Nancy Hanks, and her husband had died, leaving her with three children. She came of a better station in life than Thomas, and was a woman with an excellent mind as well as a warm and generous heart. The household goods that she brought with her to the Lincoln home filled a four-horse wagon, and not only were her own children well clothed and cared for, but she was able at once to provide little Abraham and Sarah with comforts to which they had been strangers during the whole of their young lives. Under her wise management all jealousy was avoided between the two sets of children; urged on by her stirring example, Thomas Lincoln supplied the yet unfinished cabin with floor, door, and windows, and life became more comfortable for all its inmates, contentment if not happiness reigning in the little home.

The new stepmother quickly became very fond of Abraham, and encouraged him in every way in her power to study and improve himself. The chances for this were few enough. Mr. Lincoln has left us a vivid picture of the situation. "It was," he once wrote, "a wild region, with many bears and other wild animals still in the woods. There I grew up. There were some schools, so-called, but no qualification was ever required of a teacher beyond "readin', writin', and cipherin'" to the Rule of Three. If a straggler supposed to understand Latin happened to sojourn in the neighborhood, he was looked upon as a wizard."

The school-house was a low cabin of round logs, with split logs or "puncheons" for a floor, split logs roughly leveled with an ax and set up on legs for benches, and holes cut out in the logs and the space filled in with squares of greased paper for window-panes. The main light came in through the open door. Very often Webster's "Elementary Spelling-book" was the only text-book. This was the kind of school most common in the middle West during Mr. Lincoln's boyhood, though already in some places there were schools of a more pretentious character. Indeed, back in Kentucky, at the very time that Abraham, a child of six, was learning his letters from Zachariah Riney, a boy only a year older was attending a Catholic seminary in the very next county. It is doubtful if they ever met, but the destinies of the two were strangely interwoven, for the older boy was Jefferson Davis, who became head of the Confederate government shortly after Lincoln was elected President of the United States.

As Abraham had been only seven years old when he left Kentucky, the little beginnings he learned in the schools kept by Riney and Hazel in that State must have been very slight, probably only his alphabet, or at most only three or four pages of Webster's "Elementary Spelling-book." The multiplication-table was still a mystery to him, and he could read or write only the words he spelled. His first two years in Indiana seem to have passed without schooling of any sort, and the school he attended shortly after coming under the care of his stepmother was of the simplest kind, for the Pigeon Creek settlement numbered only eight or ten poor families, and they lived deep in the forest, where, even if they had had the money for such luxuries, it would have been impossible to buy books, slates, pens, ink, or paper. It is worthy of note, however, that in our western country, even under such difficulties, a school-house was one of the first buildings to rise in every frontier settlement. Abraham's second school in Indiana was held when he was fourteen years old, and the third in his seventeenth year. By that time he had more books and better teachers, but he had to walk four or five miles to reach them. We know that he learned to write, and was provided with pen, ink, and a copy-book, and a very small supply of writing-paper, for copies have been printed of several scraps on which he carefully wrote down tables of long measure, land measure, and dry measure, as well as examples in multiplication and compound division, from his arithmetic. He was never able to go to school again after this time, and though the instruction he received from his five teachers--two in Kentucky and three in Indiana--extended over a period of nine years, it must be remembered that it made up in all less than one twelve-month; "that the aggregate of all his schooling did not amount to one year." The fact that he received this instruction, as he himself said, "by littles," was doubtless an advantage. A lazy or indifferent boy would of course have forgotten what was taught him at one time before he had opportunity at another; but Abraham was neither indifferent nor lazy, and these widely separated fragments of instruction were precious steps to self-help. He pursued his studies with very unusual purpose and determination not only to understand them at the moment, but to fix them firmly in his mind. His early companions all agree that he employed every spare moment in keeping on with some one of his studies. His stepmother tells us that "When he came across a passage that struck him, he would write it down on boards if he had no paper, and keep it there until he did get paper. Then he would rewrite it, look at it, repeat it. He had a copy-book, a kind of scrap-book, in which he put down all things, and thus preserved them." He spent long evenings doing sums on the fire-shovel. Iron fire-shovels were a rarity among pioneers. Instead they used a broad, thin clapboard with one end narrowed to a handle, arranging with this the piles of coals upon the hearth, over which they set their "skillet" and "oven" to do their cooking. It was on such a wooden shovel that Abraham worked his sums by the flickering firelight, making his figures with a piece of charcoal, and, when the shovel was all covered, taking a drawing-knife and shaving it off clean again.

The hours that he was able to devote to his penmanship, his reading, and his arithmetic were by no means many; for, save for the short time that he was actually in school, he was, during all these years, laboring hard on his father's farm, or hiring his youthful strength to neighbors who had need of help in the work of field or forest. In pursuit of his knowledge he was on an up-hill path; yet in spite of all obstacles he worked his way to so much of an education as placed him far ahead of his schoolmates and quickly abreast of his various teachers. He borrowed every book in the neighborhood. The list is a short one: "Robinson Crusoe," "Aesop's Fables," Bunyan's "Pilgrim's Progress," Weems's "Life of Washington," and a "History of the United States." When everything else had been read, he resolutely began on the "Revised Statutes of Indiana," which Dave Turnham, the constable, had in daily use, but permitted him to come to his house and read.

Though so fond of his books; it must not be supposed that he cared only for work and serious study. He was a social, sunny-tempered lad, as fond of jokes and fun as he was kindly and industrious. His stepmother said of him: "I can say, what scarcely one mother in a thousand can say, Abe never gave me a cross word or look, and never refused . . . to do anything I asked him. . . . I must say . . that Abe was the best boy I ever saw or expect to see."

He and John Johnston, his stepmother's son, and John Hanks, a relative of his own mother's, worked barefoot together in the fields, grubbing, plowing, hoeing, gathering and shucking corn, and taking part, when occasion offered, in the practical jokes and athletic exercises that enlivened the hard work of the pioneers. For both work and play Abraham had one great advantage. He was not only a tall, strong country boy: he soon grew to be a tall, strong, sinewy man. He early reached the unusual height of six feet four inches, and his long arms gave him a degree of power as an axman that few were able to rival. He therefore usually led his fellows in efforts of muscle as well as of mind. That he could outrun, outlift, outwrestle his boyish companions, that he could chop faster, split more rails in a day, carry a heavier log at a "raising," or excel the neighborhood champion in any feat of frontier athletics, was doubtless a matter of pride with him; but stronger than all else was his eager craving for knowledge. He felt instinctively that the power of using the mind rather than the muscles was the key to success. He wished not only to wrestle with the best of them, but to be able to talk like the preacher, spell and cipher like the school-master, argue like the lawyer, and write like the editor. Yet he was as far as possible from being a prig. He was helpful, sympathetic, cheerful. In all the neighborhood gatherings, when settlers of various ages came together at corn-huskings or house-raisings, or when mere chance brought half a dozen of them at the same time to the post-office or the country store, he was able, according to his years, to add his full share to the gaiety of the company. By reason of his reading and his excellent memory, he soon became the best story-teller among his companions; and even the slight training gained from his studies greatly broadened and strengthened the strong reasoning faculty with which he had been gifted by nature. His wit might be mischievous, but it was never malicious, and his nonsense was never intended to wound or to hurt the feelings. It is told of him that he added to his fund of jokes and stories humorous imitations of the sermons of eccentric preachers.

Very likely too much is made of all these boyish pranks. He grew up very like his fellows. In only one particular did he differ greatly from the frontier boys around him. He never took any pleasure in hunting. Almost every youth of the backwoods early became an excellent shot and a confirmed sportsman. The woods still swarmed with game, and every cabin depended largely upon this for its supply of food. But to his strength was added a gentleness which made him shrink from killing or inflicting pain, and the time the other boys gave to lying in ambush, he preferred to spend in reading or in efforts at improving his mind.

Only twice during his life in Indiana was the routine of his employment changed. When he was about sixteen years old he worked for a time for a man who lived at the mouth of Anderson's Creek, and here part of his duty was to manage a ferry-boat which carried passengers across the Ohio River. It was very likely this experience which, three years later, brought him another. Mr. Gentry, the chief man of the village of Gentryville that had grown up a mile or so from his father's cabin, loaded a flatboat on the Ohio River with the produce his store had collected--corn, flour, pork, bacon, and other miscellaneous provisions--and putting it in charge of his son Allen Gentry and of Abraham Lincoln, sent them with it down the Ohio and Mississippi Rivers, to sell its cargo at the plantations of the lower Mississippi, where sugar and cotton were the principal crops, and where other food supplies were needed to feed the slaves. No better proof is needed of the reputation for strength, skill, honesty, and intelligence that this tall country boy had already won for himself, than that he was chosen to navigate the flatboat a thousand miles to the "sugar-coast" of the Mississippi River, sell its load, and bring back the money. Allen Gentry was supposed to be in command, but from the record of his after life we may be sure that Abraham did his full share both of work and management. The elder Gentry paid Lincoln eight dollars a month and his passage home on a steamboat for this service. The voyage was made successfully, although not without adventure; for one night, after the boat was tied up to the shore, the boys were attacked by seven negroes, who came aboard intending to kill and rob them. There was a lively scrimmage, in which, though slightly hurt, they managed to beat off their assailants, and then, hastily cutting their boat adrift, swung out on the stream. The marauding band little dreamed that they were attacking the man who in after years was to give their race its freedom; and though the future was equally hidden from Abraham, it is hard to estimate the vistas of hope and ambition that this long journey opened to him. It was his first look into the wide, wide world.

II. CAPTAIN LINCOLN.

By this time the Lincoln homestead was no longer on the frontier. During the years that passed while Abraham was growing from a child, scarcely able to wield the ax placed in his hands, into a tall, capable youth, the line of frontier settlements had been gradually but steadily pushing on beyond Gentryville toward the Mississippi River. Every summer canvas-covered moving wagons wound their slow way over new roads into still newer country; while the older settlers, left behind, watched their progress with longing eyes. It was almost as if a spell had been cast over these toil-worn pioneers, making them forget, at sight of such new ventures, all the hardships they had themselves endured in subduing the wilderness. At last, on March 1, 1830, when Abraham was just twenty-one years old, the Lincolns, yielding to this overmastering frontier impulse to "move" westward, left the old farm in Indiana to make a new home in Illinois. "Their mode of conveyance was wagons drawn by ox-teams," Mr. Lincoln wrote in 1860; "and Abraham drove one of the teams." They settled in Macon County on the north side of the Sangamon River, about ten miles west of Decatur, where they built a cabin, made enough rails to fence ten acres of ground, fenced and cultivated the ground, and raised a crop of corn upon it that first season. It was the same heavy labor over again that they had endured when they went from Kentucky to Indiana; but this time the strength and energy of young Abraham were at hand to inspire and aid his father, and there was no miserable shivering year of waiting in a half-faced camp before the family could be suitably housed. They were not to escape hardship, however. They fell victims to fever and ague, which they had not known in Indiana, and became greatly discouraged; and the winter after their arrival proved one of intense cold and suffering for the pioneers, being known in the history of the State as "the winter of the deep snow." The severe weather began in the Christmas holidays with a storm of such fatal suddenness that people who were out of doors had difficulty in reaching their homes, and not a few perished, their fate remaining unknown until the melting snows of early spring showed where they had fallen.

In March, 1831, at the end of this terrible winter, Abraham Lincoln left his father's cabin to seek his own fortune in the world. It was the frontier custom for young men to do this when they reached the age of twenty-one. Abraham was now twenty-two, but had willingly remained with his people an extra year to give them the benefit of his labor and strength in making the new home.

He had become acquainted with a man named Offut, a trader and speculator, who pretended to great business shrewdness, but whose chief talent lay in boasting of the magnificent things he meant to do. Offut engaged Abraham, with his stepmother's son, John D. Johnston, and John Hanks, to take a flatboat from Beardstown, on the Illinois River, to New Orleans; and all four arranged to meet at Springfield as soon as the snow should melt.

In March, when the snow finally melted, the country was flooded and traveling by land was utterly out of the question. The boys, therefore, bought a large canoe, and in it floated down the Sangamon River to keep their appointment with Offut. It was in this somewhat unusual way that Lincoln made his first entry into the town whose name was afterward to be linked with his own.

Offut was waiting for them, with the discouraging news that he had been unable to get a flatboat at Beardstown. The young men promptly offered to make the flatboat, since one was not to be bought; and they set to work, felling the trees for it on the banks of the stream. Abraham's father had been a carpenter, so the use of tools was no mystery to him; and during his trip to New Orleans with Allen Gentry he had learned enough about flatboats to give him confidence in this task of shipbuilding. Neither Johnston nor Hanks was gifted with skill or industry, and it is clear that Lincoln was, from the start, leader of the party, master of construction, and captain of the craft.

The floods went down rapidly while the boat was building, and when they tried to sail their new craft it stuck midway across the dam of Rutledge's mill at New Salem, a village of fifteen or twenty houses not many miles from their starting-point. With its bow high in air, and its stern under water, it looked like some ungainly fish trying to fly, or some bird making an unsuccessful attempt to swim. The voyagers appeared to have suffered irreparable shipwreck at the very outset of their venture, and men and women came down from their houses to offer advice or to make fun of the young boatmen as they waded about in the water, with trousers rolled very high, seeking a way out of their difficulty. Lincoln's self-control and good humor proved equal to their banter, while his engineering skill speedily won their admiration. The amusement of the onlookers changed to gaping wonder when they saw him deliberately bore a hole in the bottom of the boat near the bow, after which, fixing up some kind of derrick, he tipped the boat so that the water she had taken in at the stern ran out in front, and she floated safely over the dam. This novel method of bailing a boat by boring a hole in her bottom fully established his fame at New Salem, and so delighted the enthusiastic Offut that, on the spot, he engaged its inventor to come back after the voyage to New Orleans and act as clerk for him in a store.

The hole plugged up again, and the boat's cargo reloaded, they made the remainder of the journey in safety. Lincoln returned by steamer from New Orleans to St. Louis, and from there made his way to New Salem on foot. He expected to find Offut already established in the new store, but neither he nor his goods had arrived. While "loafing about," as the citizens of New Salem expressed it, waiting for him, the newcomer had a chance to exhibit another of his accomplishments. An election was to be held, but one of the clerks, being taken suddenly ill, could not be present. Penmen were not plenty in the little town, and Mentor Graham, the other election clerk, looking around in perplexity for some one to fill the vacant place, asked young Lincoln if he knew how to write. Lincoln answered, in the lazy speech of the country, that he "could make a few rabbit tracks," and that being deemed quite sufficient, was immediately sworn in, and set about discharging the duties of his first office. The way he performed these not only gave general satisfaction, but greatly interested Mentor Graham, who was the village schoolmaster, and from that time on proved a most helpful friend to him.

Offut finally arrived with a miscellaneous lot of goods, which Lincoln opened and put in order, and the storekeeping began. Trade does not seem to have been brisk, for Offut soon increased his venture by renting the Rutledge and Cameron mill, on whose historic dam the flatboat had come to grief. For a while the care of this mill was added to Lincoln's other duties. He made himself generally useful besides, his old implement, the ax, not being entirely discarded. We are told that he cut down trees and split rails enough to make a large hogpen adjoining the mill, a performance not at all surprising when it is remembered that up to this time the greater part of his life had been spent in the open air, and that his still growing muscles must have eagerly welcomed tasks like this, which gave him once more the exercise that measuring calico and weighing out groceries failed to supply. Young Lincoln's bodily vigor stood him in good stead in many ways. In frontier life strength and athletic skill served as well for popular amusement as for prosaic toil, and at times, indeed, they were needed for personal defence. Every community had its champion wrestler, a man of considerable local importance, in whose success the neighbors took a becoming interest. There was, not far from New Salem, a settlement called Clary's Grove, where lived a set of restless, rollicking young backwoodsmen with a strong liking for frontier athletics and rough practical jokes. Jack Armstrong was the leader of these, and until Lincoln's arrival had been the champion wrestler of both Clary's Grove and New Salem. He and his friends had not the slightest personal grudge against Lincoln; but hearing the neighborhood talk about the newcomer, and especially Offut's extravagant praise of his clerk, who, according to Offut's statement, knew more than any one else in the United States, and could beat the whole county at running, jumping or "wrastling," they decided that the time had come to assert themselves, and strove to bring about a trial of strength between Armstrong and Lincoln. Lincoln, who disapproved of all this "woolling and pulling," as he called it, and had no desire to come to blows with his neighbors, put off the encounter as long as possible. At length even his good temper was powerless to avert it, and the wrestling-match took place. Jack Armstrong soon found that he had tackled a man as strong and skilful as himself; and his friends, seeing him likely to get the worst of it, swarmed to his assistance, almost succeeding, by tripping and kicking, in getting Lincoln down. At the unfairness of this Lincoln became suddenly and furiously angry, put forth his entire strength, lifted the pride of Clary's Grove in his arms like a child, and holding him high in the air, almost choked the life out of him. It seemed for a moment as though a general fight must follow; but even while Lincoln's fierce rage compelled their respect, his quickly returning self-control won their admiration, and the crisis was safely passed. Instead of becoming enemies and leaders in a neighborhood feud, as might have been expected, the two grew to be warm friends, the affection thus strangely begun lasting through life. They proved useful to each other in various ways, and years afterward Lincoln made ample amends for his rough treatment of the other's throat by saving the neck of Jack Armstrong's son from the halter in a memorable trial for murder. The Clary's Grove "boys" voted Lincoln "the cleverest fellow that had ever broke into the settlement," and thereafter took as much pride in his peaceableness and book-learning as they did in the rougher and more questionable accomplishments of their discomfited leader.

Lincoln himself was not so easily satisfied. His mind as well as his muscles hungered for work, and he confided to Mentor Graham, possibly with some diffidence, his "notion to study English grammar." Instead of laughing at him, Graham heartily encouraged the idea, saying it was the very best thing he could do. With quickened zeal Lincoln announced that if he had a grammar he would begin at once at this the schoolmaster was obliged to confess that he knew of no such book in New Salem. He thought, however, that there might be one at Vaner's, six miles away. Promptly after breakfast the next morning Lincoln set out in search of it. He brought the precious volume home in triumph, and with Graham's occasional help found no difficulty in mastering its contents. Indeed, it is very likely that he was astonished, and even a bit disappointed, to find so little mystery in it. He is reported to have said that if this was a "science," he thought he would like to begin on another one. In the eyes of the townspeople, however, it was no small achievement, and added greatly to his reputation as a scholar. There is no record of any other study commenced at this time, but it is certain that he profited much by helpful talks with Mentor Graham, and that he borrowed every book the schoolmaster's scanty library was able to furnish.

Though outwardly uneventful, this period of his life was both happy and profitable. He was busy at useful labor, was picking up scraps of schooling, was making friends and learning to prize them at their true worth; was, in short, developing rapidly from a youth into a young man. Already he began to feel stirrings of ambition which prompted him to look beyond his own daily needs toward the larger interests of his county and his State. An election for members of the Illinois legislature was to take place in August, 1832. Sangamon County was entitled to four representatives. Residents of the county over twenty-one years of age were eligible to election, and audacious as it might appear, Lincoln determined to be a candidate.

The people of New Salem, Ill., those of all other Western towns, took a keen interest in politics; "politics" meaning, in that time and place, not only who was to be President or governor, but concerning itself with questions which came much closer home to dwellers on the frontier. "Internal improvements," as they were called--the building of roads and clearing out of streams so that men and women who lived in remote places might be able to travel back and forth and carry on trade with the rest of the world-- became a burning question in Illinois. There was great need of such improvements; and in this need young Lincoln saw his opportunity.

It was by way of the Sangamon River that he entered politics. That uncertain watercourse had already twice befriended him. He had floated on it in flood-time from his father's cabin into Springfield. A few weeks later its rapidly falling waters landed him on the dam at Rutledge's mill, introducing him effectively if unceremoniously to the inhabitants of New Salem. Now it was again to play a part in his life, starting him on a political career that ended only in the White House. Surely no insignificant stream has had a greater influence on the history of a famous man. It was a winding and sluggish creek, encumbered with driftwood and choked by sand-bars; but it flowed through a country already filled with ambitious settlers, where the roads were atrociously bad, becoming in rainy seasons wide seas of pasty black mud, and remaining almost impassable for weeks at a time. After a devious course the Sangamon found its way into the Illinois River, and that in turn flowed into the Mississippi. Most of the settlers were too new to the region to know what a shallow, unprofitable stream the Sangamon really was, for the deep snows of

183031 and of the following winter had supplied it with an unusual volume of water. It was natural, therefore, that they should regard it as the heaven-sent solution of their problem of travel and traffic with the outside world. If it could only be freed from driftwood, and its channel straightened a little, they felt sure it might be used for small steamboats during a large part of the year.

The candidates for the legislature that summer staked their chances of success on the zeal they showed for "internal improvements." Lincoln was only twenty-three. He had been in the county barely nine months. Sangamon County was then considerably larger than the whole State of Rhode Island, and he was of course familiar with only a small part of it or its people; but he felt that he did know the river. He had sailed on it and been shipwrecked by it; he had, moreover, been one of a party of men and boys, armed with long-handled axes, who went out to chop away obstructions and meet a small steamer that, a few weeks earlier, had actually forced its way up from the Illinois River.

Following the usual custom, he announced his candidacy in the local newspaper in a letter dated March 9, addressed "To the People of Sangamon County." It was a straightforward, manly statement of his views on questions of the day, written in as good English as that used by the average college-bred man of his years. The larger part of it was devoted to arguments for the improvement of the Sangamon River. Its main interest for us lies in the frank avowal of his personal ambition that is contained in the closing paragraph.

"Every man is said to have his peculiar ambition," he wrote. "Whether it be true or not, I can say, for one, that I have no other so great as that of being truly esteemed of my fellowmen by rendering myself worthy of their esteem. How far I shall succeed in gratifying this ambition is yet to be developed. I am young, and unknown to many of you. I was born, and have ever remained, in the most humble walks of life. I have no wealthy or popular relations or friends to recommend me. My case is thrown exclusively upon the independent voters of the county; and if elected, they will have conferred a favor upon me for which I shall be unremitting in my labors to compensate. But if the good people in their wisdom shall see fit to keep me in the background, I have been too familiar with disappointments to be very much chagrined."

He soon had an opportunity of being useful to his fellow-men, though in a way very different from the one he was seeking. About four weeks after he had published his letter "To the People of Sangamon County," news came that Black Hawk, the veteran war-chief of the Sac Indians, was heading an expedition to cross the Mississippi River and occupy once more the lands that had been the home of his people. There was great excitement among the settlers in Northern Illinois, and the governor called for six hundred volunteers to take part in a campaign against the Indians. He met a quick response; and Lincoln, unmindful of what might become of his campaign for the legislature if he went away, was among the first to enlist. When his company met on the village green to choose their officers, three-quarters of the men, to Lincoln's intense surprise and pleasure, marched over to the spot where he was standing and grouped themselves around him, signifying in this way their wish to make him captain. We have his own word for it that no success of his after life gave him nearly as much satisfaction. On April 21, two days after the call for volunteers had been printed, the company was organized. A week later it was mustered into service, becoming part of the Fourth Illinois Mounted Volunteers, and started at once for the hostile frontier.

Lincoln's soldiering lasted about three months. He was in no battle, but there was plenty of "roughing it," and occasionally real hardship, as when the men were obliged to go for three days without food. The volunteers had not enlisted for any definite length of time, and seeing no prospect of fighting, they soon became clamorous to return home. Accordingly his and other companies were mustered out of service on May 27, at the mouth of Fox River. At the same time the governor, not wishing to weaken his forces before the arrival of other soldiers to take their places, called for volunteers to remain twenty days longer. Lincoln had gone to the frontier to do real service, not for the glory of being captain. Accordingly, on the day on which he was mustered out as an officer he re-enlisted, becoming Private Lincoln in Captain Iles's company of mounted volunteers, sometimes known as the Independent Spy Battalion. This organization appears to have been very independent indeed, not under the control of any regiment or brigade, but receiving orders directly from the commander-in-chief, and having many unusual privileges, such as freedom from all camp duties, and permission to draw rations as much and as often as they pleased. After laying down his official dignity and joining this band of privileged warriors, the campaign became much more of a holiday for the tall volunteer from New Salem. He entered with enthusiasm into all the games and athletic sports with which the soldiers beguiled the tedium of camp, and grew in popularity from beginning to end of his service. When, at length, the Independent Spy Battalion was mustered out on June 16, 1832, he started on the journey home with a merry group of his companions. He and his messmate, George M. Harrison, had the misfortune to have their horses stolen the very day before, but Harrison's record says:

"I laughed at our fate, and he joked at it, and we all started of merrily. The generous men of our company walked and rode by turns with us, and we fared about equal with the rest. But for this generosity, our legs would have had to do the better work, for in that day this dreary route furnished no horses to buy or to steal, and whether on horse or afoot, we always had company, for many of the horses' backs were too sore for riding."

Lincoln reached New Salem about the first of August, only ten days before the election. He had lost nothing in popular esteem by his prompt enlistment to defend the frontier, and his friends had been doing manful service for him; but there were by this time thirteen candidates in the field, with a consequent division of interest. When the votes were counted, Lincoln was found to be eighth on the list--an excellent showing when we remember that he was a newcomer in the county, and that he ran as a Whig, which was the unpopular party. In his own home town of New Salem only three votes had been cast against him. Flattering as all this was, the fact remained that he was defeated, and the result of the election brought him face to face with a very serious question. He was without means and without employment. Offut had failed and had gone away. What was he to do next? He thought of putting his strong muscles to account by learning the blacksmith trade; thought also of trying to become a lawyer, but feared he could not succeed at that without a better education. It was the same problem that has confronted millions of young Americans before and since. In his case there was no question which he would rather be--the only question was what success he might reasonably hope for if he tried to study law.

Before his mind was fully made up, chance served to postpone, and in the end greatly to increase his difficulty. Offut's successors in business, two brothers named Herndon, had become discouraged, and they offered to sell out to Lincoln and an acquaintance of his named William F. Berry, on credit, taking their promissory notes in payment. Lincoln and Berry could not foresee that the town of New Salem had already lived through its best days, and was destined to dwindle and grow smaller until it almost disappeared from the face of the earth. Unduly hopeful, they accepted the offer, and also bought out, on credit, two other merchants who were anxious to sell. It is clear that the flattering vote Lincoln had received at the recent election, and the confidence New Salem felt in his personal character, alone made these transactions possible, since not a dollar of actual money changed hands during all this shifting of ownership. In the long run the people's faith in him was fully justified; but meantime he suffered years of worry and harassing debt. Berry proved a worthless partner; the business a sorry failure. Seeing this, Lincoln and Berry sold out, again on credit, to the Trent brothers, who soon broke up the store and ran away. Berry also departed and died; and in the end all the notes came back upon Lincoln for payment. Of course he had not the money to meet these obligations. He did the next best thing: he promised to pay as soon as he could, and remaining where he was, worked hard at whatever he found to do. Most of his creditors, knowing him to be a man of his word, patiently bided their time, until, in the course of long years, he paid, with interest, every cent of what he used to call, in rueful satire upon his own folly, his "National Debt."

III. LAWYER LINCOLN

Unlucky as Lincoln's attempt at storekeeping had been, it served one good purpose. Indeed, in a way it may be said to have determined his whole future career. He had had a hard struggle to decide between becoming a blacksmith or a lawyer; and when chance seemed to offer a middle course, and he tried to be a merchant, the wish to study law had certainly not faded from his mind.

There is a story that while cleaning up the store, he came upon a barrel which contained, among a lot of forgotten rubbish, some stray volumes of Blackstone's "Commentaries," and that this lucky find still further quickened his interest in the law. Whether this tale be true or not it seems certain that during the time the store was running its downward course from bad to worse, he devoted a large part of his too abundant leisure to reading and study of various kinds. People who knew him then have told how he would lie for hours under a great oak-tree that grew just outside the store door, poring over his book, and "grinding around with the shade" as it shifted from north to east.

Lincoln's habit of reading was still further encouraged by his being appointed postmaster of New Salem on May 7, 1833, an office he held for about three years--until New Salem grew too small to have a post-office of its own, and the mail was sent to a neighboring town. The office was so insignificant that according to popular fable it had no fixed abiding-place, Lincoln being supposed to carry it about with him in his hat! It was, however, large enough to bring him a certain amount of consideration, and, what pleased him still better, plenty of newspapers to read-- newspapers that just then were full of the exciting debates of Clay and Webster, and other great men in Congress.

The rate of postage on letters was still twenty-five cents, and small as the earnings of the office undoubtedly were, a little change found its way now and then into his hands. In the scarcity of money on the frontier, this had an importance hard for us to realize. A portion of this money, of course, belonged to the government. That he used only what was rightfully his own we could be very sure, even if a sequel to this post office experience were not known which shows his scrupulous honesty where government funds were concerned. Years later, after he had become a practising lawyer in Springfield, an agent of the Post-office Department called upon him in his office one day to collect a balance due from the New Salem post-office, amounting to about seventeen dollars. A shade of perplexity passed over his face, and a friend, sitting by, offered to lend him the money if he did not at the moment have it with him. Without answering, Lincoln rose, and going to a little trunk that stood by the wall, opened it and took out the exact sum, carefully done up in a small package. "I never use any man's money but my own, he quietly remarked, after the agent had gone.

Soon after he was raised to the dignity of postmaster another piece of good fortune came in his way. Sangamon County covered a territory some forty miles long by fifty wide, and almost every citizen in it seemed intent on buying or selling land, laying out new roads, or locating some future city. John Calhoun, the county surveyor, therefore, found himself with far more work than he could personally attend to, and had to appoint deputies to assist him. Learning the high esteem in which Lincoln was held by the people of New Salem, he wisely concluded to make him a deputy, although they differed in politics. It was a flattering offer, and Lincoln accepted gladly. Of course he knew almost nothing about surveying, but he got a compass and chain, and, as he tells us, "studied Flint and Gibson a little, and went at it." The surveyor, who was a man of talent and education, not only gave Lincoln the appointment, but, it is said, lent him the book in which to study the art. Lincoln carried the book to his friend Mentor Graham, and "went at it" to such purpose that in six weeks he was ready to begin the practice of his new profession. Like Washington, who, it will be remembered, followed the same calling in his youth, he became an excellent surveyor.

Lincoln's store had by this time "winked out," to use his own quaint phrase; and although the surveying and his post-office supplied his daily needs, they left absolutely nothing toward paying his "National Debt." Some of his creditors began to get uneasy, and in the latter part of 1834 a man named Van Bergen, who held one of the Lincoln-Berry notes, refusing to trust him any longer, had his horse, saddle, and surveying instruments seized by the sheriff and sold at public auction, thus sweeping away the means by which, as he said, he "procured bread and kept soul and body together." Even in this strait his known honesty proved his salvation. Out of pure friendliness, James Short bought in the property and gave it back to the young surveyor, allowing him time to repay.

It took Lincoln seventeen years to get rid of his troublesome "National Debt," the last instalment not being paid until after his return from his term of service in Congress at Washington; but it was these seventeen years of industry, rigid economy, and unflinching fidelity to his promises that earned for him the title of "Honest Old Abe," which proved of such inestimable value to himself and his country.

During all this time of trial and disappointment he never lost his courage, his steady, persevering industry, or his determination to succeed. He was not too proud to accept any honest employment that offered itself. He would go into the harvest-field and work there when other tasks were not pressing, or use his clerkly hand to straighten up a neglected ledger; and his lively humor, as well as his industry, made him a welcome guest at any farm-house in the county. Whatever he might be doing, he was never too busy to help a neighbor. His strong arm was always at the service of the poor and needy.

Two years after his defeat for the legislature there was another election. His friends and acquaintanceS in the county had increased, and, since he had received such a flattering vote the first time, it was but natural that he should wish to try again. He began his campaign in April, giving himself full three months for electioneering. It was customary in those days for candidates to attend all manner of neighborhood gatherings--"raisings" of new cabins, horseraces, shooting-matches, auctions--anything that served to call the settlers together; and it was social popularity, quite as much as ability to discuss political questions, that carried weight with such assemblies. Lincoln, it is needless to say, was in his element. He might be called upon to act as judge in a horse-race, or to make a speech upon the Constitution! He could do both. As a laughing peacemaker between two quarrelsome patriots he had no equal; and as contestant in an impromptu match at quoit-throwing, or lifting heavy weights, his native tact and strong arm served him equally well. Candidates also visited farms and outlying settlements, where they were sometimes unexpectedly called upon to show their mettle and muscle in more useful labor. One farmer has recorded how Lincoln "came to my house near Island Grove during harvest. There were some thirty men in the field. He got his dinner, and went out in the field where the men were at work. I gave him an introduction, and the boys said that they could not vote for a man unless he could make a hand. 'Well, boys,' said he, "if that is all, I am sure of your votes.' He took hold of the cradle and led the way all the round with perfect ease. The boys were satisfied, and I don't think he lost a vote in the crowd."

Sometimes two or more candidates would meet at such places, and short speeches would be called for and given, the harvesters throwing down their scythes meanwhile to listen, and enlivening the occasion with keen criticisms of the method and logic of the rival orators. Altogether the campaign was more spirited than that of two years before. Again there were thirteen candidates for the four places; but this time, when the election was over, it was found that only one man in the long list had received more votes than Abraham Lincoln.

Lincoln's election to the legislature of Illinois in August, 1834, marks the end of the pioneer period of his life. He was done now with the wild carelessness of the woods, with the rough jollity of Clary's Grove, with odd jobs for his daily bread--with all the details of frontier poverty. He continued for years to be a very poor man, harassed by debts he was constantly laboring to pay, and sometimes absolutely without money: but from this time on he met and worked with men of wider knowledge and better-trained minds than those he had known in Gentryville and New Salem, while the simple social life of Vandalia, where he went to attend the sessions of the legislature, was more elegant than anything he had yet seen.

It must be frankly admitted that his success at this election was a most important event in his life. Another failure might have discouraged even his hopeful spirit, and sent him to the blacksmith-shop to make wagon-tires and shoe horses for the balance of his days. With this flattering vote to his credit, however, he could be very sure that he had made a wise choice between the forge and the lawyer's desk. At first he did not come into special notice in the legislature. He wore, according to the custom of the time, a decent suit of blue jeans, and was known simply as a rather quiet young man, good-natured and sensible. Soon people began to realize that he was a man to be reckoned with in the politics of the county and State. He was reelected in 1836, 1838, and 1840, and thus for eight years had a full share in shaping the public laws of Illinois. The Illinois legislature may indeed be called the school wherein he learned that extraordinary skill and wisdom in statesmanship which he exhibited in later years. In 1838 and 1840 all the Whig members of the Illinois House of Representatives gave him their vote for Speaker, but, the Democrats being in a majority, could not elect him.

His campaign expenses were small enough to suit the most exacting. It is recorded that at one time some of the leading Whigs made up a purse of two hundred dollars to pay his personal expenses. After the election he returned the sum of $199.25, with the request that it be given back to the subscribers. "I did not need the money," he explained. "I made the canvass on my own horse; my entertainment, being at the houses of friends, cost me nothing; and my only outlay was seventy-five cents for a barrel of cider, which some farm-hands insisted I should treat them to."

One act of his while a member of the legislature requires special mention because of the great events of his after-life. Even at that early date, nearly a quarter of a century before the beginning of the Civil War, slavery was proving a cause of much trouble and ill-will. The "abolitionists," as the people were called who wished the slaves to be free, and the "pro-slavery" men, who approved of keeping them in bondage, had already come to wordy war. Illinois was a free State, but many of its people preferred slavery, and took every opportunity of making their wishes known. In 1837 the legislature passed a set of resolutions "highly disapproving abolition societies." Lincoln and five others voted against it; but, not content with this, Lincoln also drew up a paper protesting against the passage of such a resolution and stating his views on slavery. They were not extreme views. Though declaring slavery to be an evil, he did not insist that the black people ought to be set free. But so strong was the popular feeling against anything approaching "abolitionism" that only one man out of the five who voted against the resolution had the courage to sign this protest with him. Lincoln was young, poor, and in need of all the good-will at his command. Nobody could have blamed him for leaving it unwritten; yet he felt the wrong of slavery so keenly that he could not keep silent merely because the views he held happened to be unpopular; and this protest, signed by him and Dan Stone, has come down to us, the first notable public act in the great career that made his name immortal.

During the eight years that he was in the legislature he had been working away at the law. Even before his first election his friend John T. Stuart, who had been major of volunteers in the Black Hawk War while Lincoln was captain, and who, like Lincoln, had reenlisted in the Independent Spy Battalion, had given him hearty encouragement. Stuart was now practising law in. Springfield. After the campaign was over, Lincoln borrowed the necessary books of Stuart, and entered upon the study in good earnest. According to his own statement, "he studied with nobody. . . . In the autumn of 1836 he obtained a law license, and on April 15, 1837, removed to Springfield and commenced the practice, his old friend Stuart taking him into partnership."

Lincoln had already endeared himself to the people of Springfield by championing a project they had much at heart--the removal of the State capital from Vandalia to their own town. This was accomplished, largely through his efforts, about the time he went to Springfield to live. This change from New Salem, a village of fifteen or twenty houses, to a "city" of two thousand inhabitants, placed him once more in striking new relations as to dress, manners, and society. Yet, as in the case of his removal from his father's cabin to New Salem six years earlier, the change was not so startling as would at first appear. In spite of its larger population and its ambition as the new State capital, Springfield was at that time in many ways no great improvement upon New Salem. It had no public buildings, its streets and sidewalks were still unpaved, and business of all kinds was laboring under the burden of hard times.

As for himself, although he now owned a license to practise law, it was still a question how well he would succeed--whether his rugged mind and firm purpose could win him the livelihood he desired, or whether, after all, he would be forced to turn his strong muscles to account in earning his daily bread. Usually so hopeful, there were times when he was greatly depressed. His friend William Butler relates how, as they were riding together on horseback from Vandalia to Springfield at the close of a session of the legislature, Lincoln, in one of these gloomy moods, told him of the almost hopeless prospect that lay immediately before him. The session was over, his salary was all drawn, the money all spent; he had no work, and did not know where to turn to earn even a week's board. Butler bade him be of good cheer, and, kind practical friend that he was, took him and his belongings to his own home, keeping him there for a time as his guest. His most intimate friend of those days, Joshua F. Speed, tells us that soon after riding into the new capital on a borrowed horse, with all his earthly possessions packed in a pair of saddle-bags, Lincoln entered the store owned by Speed, the saddle-bags over his arm, to ask the price of a single bed with its necessary coverings and pillows. His question being answered, he remarked that very likely that was cheap enough, but, small as the price was, he was unable to pay it; adding that if Speed was willing to credit him until Christmas, and his experiment as a lawyer proved a success, he would pay then. "If I fail in this," he said sadly, "I do not know that I can ever pay you." Speed thought he had never seen such a sorrowful face. He suggested that instead of going into debt, Lincoln might share his own roomy quarters over the store, assuring him that if he chose to accept the offer, he would be very welcome. "Where is your room ?" Lincoln asked quickly. "Upstairs," and the young merchant pointed to a flight of winding steps leading from the store to the room overhead.

Lincoln picked up the saddle-bags, went upstairs, set them down on the floor, and reappeared a moment later, beaming with pleasure. "Well, Speed," he exclaimed, "I am moved!" It is seldom that heartier, truer friendships come to a man than came to Lincoln in the course of his life. On the other hand, no one ever deserved better of his fellow-men than he did; and it is pleasant to know that such brotherly aid as Butler and Speed were able to give him, offered in all sincerity and accepted in a spirit that left no sense of galling obligation on either side, helped the young lawyer over present difficulties and made it possible for him to keep on in the career he had marked out for himself.

The lawyer who works his way up from a five-dollar fee in a suit before a justice of the peace, to a five-thousand-dollar fee before the Supreme Court of his State, has a long and hard path to climb. Lincoln climbed this path for twenty-five years, with industry, perseverance, patience--above all, with that self-control and keen sense of right and wrong which always clearly traced the dividing line between his duty to his client and his duty to society and truth. His perfect frankness of statement assured him the confidence of judge and jury in every argument. His habit of fully admitting the weak points in his case gained him their close attention to his strong ones, and when clients brought him questionable cases his advice was always not to bring suit.

"Yes," he once said to a man who offered him such a case; "there is no reasonable doubt but that I can gain your case for you. I can set a whole neighborhood at loggerheads; I can distress a widowed mother and her six fatherless children, and thereby gain for you six hundred dollars, which rightfully belongs, it appears to me, as much to them as it does to you. I shall not take your case, but I will give you a little advice for nothing. You seem a sprightly, energetic man. I would advise you to try your hand at making six hundred dollars in some other way.

He would have nothing to do with the "tricks" of the profession, though he met these readily enough when practised by others. He never knowingly undertook a case in which justice was on the side of his opponent. That same inconvenient honesty which prompted him, in his store-keeping days, to close the shop and go in search of a woman he had innocently defrauded of a few ounces of tea while weighing out her groceries, made it impossible for him to do his best with a poor case. "Swett," he once exclaimed, turning suddenly to his associate, "the man is guilty; you defend him--I can't," and gave up his share of a large fee.

After his death some notes were found, written in his own hand, that had evidently been intended for a little lecture or talk to law students. They set forth forcibly, in a few words, his idea of what a lawyer ought to be and to do. He earnestly commends diligence in study, and, after diligence, promptness in keeping up the work. "As a general rule, never take your whole fee in advance," he says, "nor any more than a small retainer. When fully paid beforehand you are more than a common mortal if you can feel the same interest in the case as if something were still in prospect for you as well as for your client." Speech-making should be practised and cultivated. "It is the lawyer's avenue to the public. However able and faithful he may be in other respects, people are slow to bring him business if he cannot make a speech. And yet, there is not a more fatal error to young lawyers than relying too much on speech-making. If any one, upon his rare powers of speaking, shall claim an exemption from the drudgery of the law, his case is a failure in advance." Discourage going to law. "Persuade your neighbors to compromise whenever you can. Point out to them how the nominal winner is often a real loser--in fees, expenses, and waste of time. As a peacemaker the lawyer has a superior opportunity of being a good man. There will still be business enough." "There is a vague popular belief that lawyers are necessarily dishonest. Let no young man choosing the law for a calling for a moment yield to the popular belief. Resolve to be honest at all events; and if, in your own judgment, you cannot be an honest lawyer, resolve to be honest without being a lawyer. Choose some other occupation rather than one in the choosing of which you do, in advance, consent to be a knave."

While becoming a lawyer, Lincoln still remained a politician. In those early days in the West, the two occupations went hand in hand, almost of necessity. Laws had to be newly made to fit the needs of the new settlements, and therefore a large proportion of lawyers was sent to the State legislature. In the summer these same lawyers went about the State, practising before the circuit courts, Illinois being divided into what were called judicial circuits, each taking in several counties, and sometimes covering territory more than a hundred miles square. Springfield and the neighboring towns were in the eighth judicial circuit. Twice a year the circuit judge traveled from one county-seat to another, the lawyers who had business before the court following also.

As newspapers were neither plentiful nor widely read, members of the legislature were often called upon, while on these journeys, to explain the laws they had helped to make during the previous winter, and thus became the political teachers of the people. They had to be well informed and watchful. When, like Mr. Lincoln, they were witty, and had a fund of interesting stories besides, they were sure of a welcome and a hearing in the courtroom, or in the social gatherings that roused the various little towns during "court-week" into a liveliness quite put of the common. The tavern would be crowded to its utmost--the judge having the best room, and the lawyers being put in what was left, late comers being lucky to find even a sleeping-place on the floor. When not occupied in court, or preparing cases for the morrow, they would sit in the public room, or carry their chairs out on the sidewalk in front, exchanging stories and anecdotes, or pieces of political wisdom, while men from the town and surrounding farms, dropping in on one pretext or another, found excuse to linger and join in the talk. At meal-times the judge presided at the head of the long hotel table, on which the food was abundant if not always wholesome, and around which lawyers, jurors, witnesses, prisoners out on bail, and the men who drove the teams, gathered in friendly equality. Stories of what Mr. Lincoln did and said on the eighth judicial circuit are still quoted almost with the force of law; for in this close companionship men came to know each other thoroughly, and were judged at their true value professionally, as well as for their power to entertain.

It was only in worldly wealth that Lincoln was poor. He could hold his own with the best on the eighth judicial circuit, or anywhere else in the State. He made friends wherever he went. In politics, in daily conversation, in his work as a lawyer, his life was gradually broadening. Slowly but surely, too, his gifts as an attractive public speaker were becoming known. In 1837 he wrote and delivered an able address before the Young Men's Lyceum of Springfield. In December, 1839, Stephen A. Douglas, the most brilliant of the young Democrats then in Springfield, challenged the young Whigs of the town to a tournament of political speech-making, in which Lincoln bore a full and successful share.

The man who could not pay a week's board bill was again elected to the legislature, was invited to public banquets and toasted by name, became a popular speaker, moved in the best society of the new capital, and made, as his friends and neighbors declared, a brilliant marriage.

IV. CONGRESSMAN LINCOLN

Hopeful and cheerful as he ordinarily seemed, there was in Mr. Lincoln's disposition a strain of deep melancholy. This was not peculiar to him alone, for the pioneers as a race were somber rather than gay. Their lives had been passed for generations under the most trying physical conditions, near malaria-infested streams, and where they breathed the poison of decaying vegetation. Insufficient shelter, storms, the cold of winter, savage enemies, and the cruel labor that killed off all but the hardiest of them, had at the same time killed the happy-go-lucky gaiety of an easier form of life. They were thoughtful, watchful, wary; capable indeed of wild merriment: but it has been said that although a pioneer might laugh, he could not easily be made to smile. Lincoln's mind was unusually sound and sane and normal. He had a cheerful, wholesome, sunny nature, yet he had inherited the strongest traits of the pioneers, and there was in him, moreover, much of the poet, with a poet's great capacity for joy and pain. It is not strange that as he developed into manhood, especially when his deeper nature began to feel the stirrings of ambition and of love, these seasons of depression and gloom came upon him with overwhelming force.

During his childhood he had known few women, save his mother, and that kind, God-fearing woman his stepmother, who did so much to make his childhood hopeful and happy. No man ever honored women more truly than did Abraham Lincoln; while all the qualities that caused men to like him--his strength, his ambition, his kindliness--served equally to make him a favorite with them. In the years of his young manhood three women greatly occupied his thoughts. The first was the slender, fair-haired Ann Rutledge, whom he very likely saw for the first time as she stood with the group of mocking people on the river-bank, near her father's mill, the day Lincoln's flatboat stuck on the dam at New Salem. It was her death, two years before he went to live at Springfield, that brought on the first attack of melancholy of which we know, causing him such deep grief that for a time his friends feared his sorrow might drive him insane.

Another friend was Mary Owens, a Kentucky girl, very different from the gentle, blue-eyed Ann Rutledge, but worthy in every way of a man's affections. She had visited her sister in New Salem several years before, and Lincoln remembered her as a tall, handsome, well-educated young woman, who could be serious as well as gay, and who was considered wealthy. In the autumn of 1836, her sister, Mrs. Able, then about to start on a visit to Kentucky, jokingly offered to bring Mary back if Lincoln would promise to marry her. He, also in jest, agreed to do so. Much to his astonishment, he learned, a few months later, that she had actually returned with Mrs. Able, and his sensitive conscience made him feel that the jest had turned into real earnest, and that he was in duty bound to keep his promise if she wished him to do so. They had both changed since they last met; neither proved quite pleasing to the other, yet an odd sort of courtship was kept up, until, some time after Lincoln went to live in Springfield, Miss Owens put an end to the affair by refusing him courteously but firmly. Meantime he lived through much unhappiness and uncertainty of spirit, and made up his mind "never again to think of marrying": a resolution which he kept-- until another Kentucky girl drove it from his thoughts.

Springfield had by this time become very lively and enterprising. There was a deal of "flourishing around in carriages," as Lincoln wrote Miss Owens, and business and politics and society all played an active part in the life of the little town. The meetings of the legislature brought to the new capital a group of young men of unusual talent and ability. There was friendly rivalry between them, and party disputes ran high, but social good-humor prevailed, and the presence of these brilliant young people, later to become famous as Presidential candidates, cabinet ministers, senators, congressmen, orators, and battle heroes, lent to the social gatherings of Springfield a zest rarely found in larger places.

Into the midst of this gaiety came Mary Todd of Kentucky, twenty-one years old, handsome, accomplished and witty--a dashing and fascinating figure in dress and conversation. She was the sister of Mrs. Ninian W. Edwards, whose husband was a prominent Whig member of the legislature--one of the "Long Nine," as these men were known. Their added height was said to be fifty-five feet, and they easily made up in influence what they lacked in numbers. Lincoln was the "tallest" of them all in body and in mind, and although as poor as a church mouse, was quite as welcome anywhere as the men who wore ruffled shirts and could carry gold watches. Miss Todd soon singled out and held the admiration of such of the Springfield beaux as pleased her somewhat wilful fancy, and Lincoln, being much at the Edwards house, found himself, almost before he knew it, entangled in a new love-affair. In the course of a twelvemonth he was engaged to marry her, but something, nobody knows what or how, happened to break the engagement, and to plunge him again in a very sea of wretchedness. Nor is it necessary that we should know about it further than that a great trouble came upon him, which he bore nobly, after his kind. Few men have had his stern sense of duty, his tenderness of heart, his conscience, so easy toward others, so merciless toward himself. The trouble preyed upon his mind until he could think of nothing else. He became unable to attend to business, or to take any part in the life around him. Fearing for his reason as well as for his health if this continued, his good friend Joshua F. Speed carried him off, whether he wished or no, for a visit to his own home in Kentucky. Here they stayed for some time, and Lincoln grew much better, returning to Springfield about midsummer, almost his old self, though far from happy.

An affair that helped to bring the lovers together again is so out of keeping with the rest of his life, that it would deserve mention "for that reason, if for no other. This is nothing less than Lincoln's first and only duel. It happened that James Shields, afterward a general in two wars and a senator from two States, was at that time auditor of the State of Illinois, with his office at Springfield. He was a Democrat, and an Irishman by birth, with an Irishman's quick temper and readiness to take offense. He had given orders about collecting certain taxes which displeased the Whigs, and shortly after Lincoln came back from

Kentucky a series of humorous letters ridiculing the auditor and his order appeared in the Springfield paper, to the great amusement of the townspeople and the fury of Shields. These letters were dated from the "Lost Townships," and were supposed to be written by a farmer's widow signing herself "Aunt Rebecca." The real writers were Miss Todd and a clever friend, who undertook them more for the purpose of poking fun at Shields than for party effect. In framing the political part of their attack, they had found it necessary to consult Lincoln, and he obligingly set them a pattern by writing the first letter himself.

Shields sent to the editor of the paper to find out the name of the real "Rebecca." The editor, as in duty bound, consulted Lincoln, and was told to give Lincoln's name, but not to mention the ladies. Shields then sent Lincoln an angry challenge; and Lincoln, who considered the whole affair ridiculous, and would willingly have explained his part in it if Shields had made a gentlemanly inquiry, chose as weapons "broadswords of the largest size," and named as conditions of the duel that a plank ten feet long be firmly fixed on edge in the ground, as a line over which neither combatant was to pass his foot upon forfeit of his life. Next, lines were to be drawn upon the ground on each side of the plank, parallel with it, at the distance of the whole length of the sword and three feet additional. The passing of his own line by either man was to be deemed a surrender of the fight.

It is easy to see from these conditions that Lincoln refused to consider the matter seriously, and determined to treat it as absurdly as it deserved. He and Shields, and their respective seconds, with the broadswords, hurried away to an island in the Mississippi River, opposite Alton; but long before the plank was set up, or swords were drawn, mutual friends took the matter out of the hands of the seconds, and declared a settlement of the difficulty.

The affair created much talk and merriment in Springfield, but Lincoln found in it more than comedy. By means of it he and Miss Todd were again brought together in friendly interviews, and on November 4, they were married at the house of Mr. Edwards. Four children were born of this marriage: Robert Todd Lincoln, August 1, 1843; Edward Baker Lincoln, March 10, 1846; William

Wallace Lincoln, December 21, 1850; and Thomas Lincoln, April 4, 1853. Edward died while a baby; William, in the White House, February 20, 1862; Thomas in Chicago, July 15, 1871; and the mother, Mary Lincoln, in Springfield, July 16, 1882. Robert Lincoln was graduated from Harvard during the Civil War, serving afterward on the staff of General Grant. He has since been Secretary of War and Minister to England, and has held many other important positions of trust.

His wedding over, Lincoln took up again the practical routine of daily life. He and his bride were so poor that they could not make the visit to Kentucky that both would so much have enjoyed. They could not even set up a little home of their own. "We are not keeping house," he wrote to a friend, "but boarding at the Globe Tavern," where, he added, their room and board only cost them four dollars a week. His "National Debt" of the old New Salem days was not yet all paid off, and patiently and resolutely he went on practising the economy he had learned in the hard school of experience.

Lincoln's law partnership with John T. Stuart had lasted four years. Then Stuart was elected to Congress, and another one was formed with Judge Stephen T. Logan. It was a well-timed and important change. Stuart had always cared more for politics than for law. With Logan law was the main object, and under his guidance and encouragement Lincoln entered upon the study and practical work of his profession in a more serious spirit than ever before. His interest in politics continued, however, and in truth his practice at that time was so small as to leave ample time for both. Stuart had been twice elected to Congress, and very naturally Lincoln, who served his party quite as faithfully, and was fully as well known, hoped for a similar honor. He had profited greatly by the companionship and friendly rivalry of the talented young men of Springfield, but their talent made the prize he wished the harder to gain. Twice he was disappointed, the nomination going to other men; but in May, 1846, he was nominated, and in August of the same year elected, to the Thirtieth Congress. He had the distinction of being the only Whig member from his State, the other Illinois congressmen at that time all being Democrats; but he proved no exception to the general rule that a man rarely comes into notice during his first term in the National House of Representatives. A new member has much to learn, even when, like Lincoln, long service in a State legislature has taught him how the business of making laws is carried on. He must find out what has been done and is likely to be done on a multitude of subjects new to him, must make the acquaintance of his fellow-members, must visit the departments of government almost daily to look after the interests of people from his State and congressional district. Legally he is elected for a term of two years. Practically a session of five or six months during the first year, and of three months during the second, further reduce his opportunities more than one-half.

Lincoln did not attempt to shine forth in debate, either by a stinging retort, or burst of inspired eloquence. He went about his task quietly and earnestly, performing his share of duty with industry and a hearty admiration for the ability of better-known members. "I just take my pen," he wrote enthusiastically to a friend after listening to a speech which pleased him much, "to say that Mr. Stephens, of Georgia, is a little slim, pale-faced consumptive man, with a voice like Logan's, has just concluded the very best speech of an hour's length I ever heard. My old withered, dry eyes are full of tears yet."

During the first session of his term Lincoln made three long speeches, carefully prepared and written out beforehand. He was neither elated nor dismayed at the result. "As to speech-making," he wrote William H. Herndon, who had now become his law partner, "I find speaking here and elsewhere about the same thing. I was about as badly scared, and no worse, as I am when I speak in court."

The next year he made no set speeches, but in addition to the usual work of a congressman occupied himself with a bill that had for its object the purchase and freeing of all slaves in the District of Columbia. Slavery was not only lawful at the national capital at that time: there was, to quote Mr. Lincoln's own graphic words, "in view from the windows of the Capitol a sort of negro livery-stable, where droves of negroes were collected, temporarily kept, and finally taken to Southern markets, precisely like droves of horses."

To Lincoln and to other people who disapproved of slavery, the idea of human beings held in bondage under the very shadow of the dome of the Capitol seemed indeed a bitter mockery. As has already been stated, he did not then believe Congress had the right to interfere with slavery in States that chose to have it; but in the District of Columbia the power of Congress was supreme, and the matter was entirely different. His bill provided that the Federal Government should pay full value to the slave-holders of the District for all slaves in their possession, and should at once free the older ones. The younger ones were to be apprenticed for a term of years, in order to make them self-supporting, after which they also were to receive their freedom. The bill was very carefully thought out, and had the approval of residents of the District who held the most varied views upon slavery; but good as it was, the measure was never allowed to come to a vote, and Lincoln went back to Springfield, at the end of his term, feeling doubtless that his efforts in behalf of the slaves had been all in vain.

While in Washington he lived very simply and quietly, taking little part in the social life of the city, though cordially liked by all who made his acquaintance. An inmate of the modest boarding-house where he had rooms has told of the cheery atmosphere he seemed to bring with him into the common dining-room, where political arguments were apt to run high. He never appeared anxious to insist upon his own views; and when others, less considerate, forced matters until the talk threatened to become too furious, he would interrupt with an anecdote or a story that cleared the air and ended the discussion in a general laugh. Sometimes for exercise he would go into a bowling-alley close by, entering into the game with great zest, and accepting defeat and victory with equal good-nature. By the time he had finished a little circle would be gathered around him, enjoying his enjoyment, and laughing at his quaint expressions and sallies of wit.

His gift for jest and story-telling has become traditional. Indeed, almost every good story that has been invented within a hundred years has been laid at his door. As a matter of fact, though he was fond of telling "them, and told them well, he told comparatively few of the number that have been credited to him. He had a wonderful memory, and a fine power of making his hearers see the scene he wished to depict; but the final charm of his stories lay in their aptness, and in the kindly humor that left no sting behind it.

During his term in Congress the Presidential campaign of 1848 came on. Lincoln took an active part in the nomination and election of General Zachary Taylor--"Old Rough and Ready," as he was called--making speeches in Maryland and Massachusetts, as well as in his own home district of Illinois. Two letters that he wrote during this campaign have special interest for young readers, for they show the sympathetic encouragement he gave to young men anxious to make a place and a name for themselves in American politics.

"Now as to the young men, he wrote. "You must not wait to be brought forward by the older men. For instance, do you suppose that I should ever have got into notice if I had waited to be hunted up and pushed forward by older men? You young men get together and form a 'Rough and Ready' club, and have regular meetings and speeches. . . . Let every one play the part he can play best--some speak, some sing, and all 'holler.' Your meetings will be of evenings; the older men, and the women, will go to hear you; so that it will not only contribute to the election of 'Old Zach,' but will be an interesting pastime, and improving to the intellectual faculties of all engaged."

In another letter, answering a young friend who complained of being neglected, he said:

"Nothing could afford me more satisfaction than to learn that you and others of my young friends at home are doing battle in the contest and taking a stand far above any I have ever been able to reach. . . . I cannot conceive that other old men feel differently. Of course I cannot demonstrate what I say; but I was young once, and I am sure I was never ungenerously thrust back. I hardly know what to say. The way for a young man to rise is to improve himself every way he can, never suspecting that anybody wishes to hinder him. Allow me to assure you that suspicion and jealousy never did help any man in any situation. There may sometimes be ungenerous attempts to keep a young man down; and they will succeed, too, if he allows his mind to be diverted from its true channel to brood over the attempted injury. Cast about and see if this feeling has not injured every person you have ever known to fall into it."

He was about forty years old when he wrote this letter. By some people that is not considered a very great age; but he doubtless felt himself immensely older, as he was infinitely wiser, than his petulant young correspondent.

General Taylor was triumphantly elected, and it then became Lincoln's duty, as Whig member of Congress from Illinois, to recommend certain persons to fill government offices in that State. He did this after he returned to Springfield, for his term in Congress ended on March 4, 1849, the day that General Taylor became President. The letters that he sent to Washington when forwarding the papers and applications of people who wished appointment were both characteristic and amusing; for in his desire not to mislead or to do injustice to any man, they were very apt to say more in favor of the men he did not wish to see appointed than in recommendation of his own particular candidates.

This absolute and impartial fairness to friend and foe alike was one of his strongest traits, governing every action of his life. If it had not been for this, he might possibly have enjoyed another term in Congress, for there had been talk of reelecting him. In spite of his confession to Speed that "being elected to Congress, though I am very grateful to our friends for having done it, has not pleased me as much as I expected," this must have been flattering. But there were many able young men in Springfield who coveted the honor, and they had entered into an agreement among themselves that each would be content with a single term. Lincoln of course remained faithful to this promise. His strict keeping of promises caused him also to lose an appointment from President Taylor as Commissioner of the General Land Office, which might easily have been his, but for which he had agreed to recommend some other Illinois man. A few weeks later the President offered to make him governor of the new Territory of Oregon. This attracted him much more than the other office had done, but he declined because his wife was unwilling to live in a place so far away.

His career in Congress, while adding little to his fame at the time, proved of great advantage to him in after life, for it gave him a close knowledge of the workings of the Federal Government, and brought him into contact with political leaders from all parts of the Union.

V. THE CHAMPION OF FREEDOM

For four or five years after his return from Congress, Lincoln remained in Springfield, working industriously at his profession. He was offered a law partnership in Chicago, but declined on the ground that his health would not stand the confinement of a great city. His business increased in volume and importance as the months went by; and it was during this time that he engaged in what is perhaps the most dramatic as well as the best known of all his law cases--his defense of Jack Armstrong's son on a charge of murder. A knot of young men had quarreled one night on the outskirts of a camp-meeting, one was killed, and suspicion pointed strongly toward young Armstrong as the murderer. Lincoln, for old friendship's sake, offered to defend him--an offer most gratefully accepted by his family. The principal witness swore that he had seen young Armstrong strike the fatal blow--had seen him distinctly by the light of a bright moon. Lincoln made him repeat the statement until it seemed as if he were sealing the death-warrant of the prisoner. Then Lincoln began his address to the jury. He was not there as a hired attorney, he told them, but because of friendship. He told of his old relations with Jack Armstrong, of the kindness the prisoner's mother had shown him in New Salem, how he had himself rocked the prisoner to sleep when the latter was a little child. Then he reviewed the testimony, pointing out how completely everything depended on the statements of this one witness; and ended by proving beyond question that his testimony was false, since, according to the almanac, which he produced in court and showed to judge and jury, THERE WAS NO MOON IN THE SKY THAT NIGHT at the hour the murder was committed. The jury brought in a verdict of "Not guilty," and the prisoner was discharged.

Lincoln was always strong with a jury. He knew how to handle men, and he had a direct way of going to the heart of things. He had, moreover, unusual powers of mental discipline. It was after his return from Congress, when he had long been acknowledged one of the foremost lawyers of the State, that he made up his mind he lacked the power of close and sustained reasoning, and set himself like a schoolboy to study works of logic and mathematics to remedy the defect. At this time he committed to memory six books of the propositions of Euclid; and, as always, he was an eager reader on many subjects, striving in this way to make up for the lack of education he had had as a boy. He was always interested in mechanical principles and their workings, and in May, 1849, patented a device for lifting vessels over shoals, which had evidently been dormant in his mind since the days of his early Mississippi River experiences. The little model of a boat, whittled out with his own hand, that he sent to the Patent Office when he filed his application, is still shown to visitors, though the invention itself failed to bring about any change in steamboat architecture.

In work and study time slipped away. He was the same cheery companion as of old, much sought after by his friends, but now more often to be found in his office surrounded by law-books and papers than had been the case before his term in Congress. His interest in politics seemed almost to have ceased when, in 1854, something happened to rouse that and his sense of right and justice as they had never been roused before. This was the repeal of the "Missouri Compromise," a law passed by Congress in the year 1820, allowing Missouri to enter the Union as a slave State, but positively forbidding slavery in all other territory of the United States lying north of latitude 36 degrees 30 minutes, which was the southern boundary-line of Missouri.

Up to that time the Southern States, where slavery was lawful, had been as wealthy and quite as powerful in politics as the Northern or free States. The great unoccupied territory lying to the west, which, in years to come, was sure to be filled with people and made into new States, lay, however, mostly north of 36 degrees 30 minutes; and it was easy to see that as new free States came one after the other into the Union the importance of the South must grow less and less, because there was little or no territory left out of which slave States could be made to offset them. The South therefore had been anxious to have the Missouri Compromise repealed.

The people of the North, on the other hand, were not all wise or disinterested in their way of attacking slavery. As always happens, self-interest and moral purpose mingled on both sides; but, as a whole, it may be said that they wished to get rid of slavery because they felt it to be wrong, and totally out of place in a country devoted to freedom and liberty. The quarrel between them was as old as the nation, and it had been gaining steadily in intensity. At first only a few persons in each section had been really interested. By the year 1850 it had come to be a question of much greater moment, and during the ten years that followed was to increase in bitterness until it absorbed the thoughts of the entire people, and plunged the country into a terrible civil war.

Abraham Lincoln had grown to manhood while the question was gaining in importance. As a youth, during his flatboat voyages to New Orleans he had seen negroes chained and beaten, and the injustice of slavery had been stamped upon his soul. The uprightness of his mind abhorred a system that kept men in bondage merely because they happened to be black. The intensity of his feeling on the subject had made him a Whig when, as a friendless boy, he lived in a town where Whig ideas were much in disfavor. The same feeling, growing stronger as he grew older, had inspired the Lincoln-Stone protest and the bill to free the slaves in the District of Columbia, and had caused him to vote at least forty times against slavery in one form or another during his short term in Congress. The repeal of the Missouri Compromise, throwing open once more to slavery a vast amount of territory from which it had been shut out, could not fail to move him deeply. His sense of justice and his strong powers of reasoning were equally stirred, and from that time until slavery came to its end through his own act, he gave his time and all his energies to the cause of freedom.

Two points served to make the repeal of the Missouri Compromise of special interest to Lincoln. The first was personal, in that the man who championed the measure, and whose influence in Congress alone made it possible, was Senator Stephen A. Douglas, who had been his neighbor in Illinois for many years.

The second was deeper. He realized that the struggle meant much more than the freedom or bondage of a few million black men: that it was in reality a struggle for the central idea of our American republic--the statement in our Declaration of Independence that "all men are created equal." He made no public speeches until autumn, but in the meantime studied the question with great care, both as to its past history and present state. When he did speak it was with a force and power that startled Douglas and, it is said, brought him privately to Lincoln with the proposition that neither of them should address a public meeting again until after the next election.

Douglas was a man of great ambition as well as of unusual political skill. Until recently he had been heartily in favor of keeping slavery out of the Northwest Territory; but he had set his heart upon being President of the United States, and he thought that he saw a chance of this if he helped the South to repeal the Missouri Compromise, and thus gained its gratitude and its votes. Without hesitation he plunged into the work and labored successfully to overthrow this law of more than thirty years' standing.

Lincoln's speech against the repeal had made a deep impression in Illinois, where he was at once recognized as the people's spokesman in the cause of freedom. His statements were so clear, his language so eloquent, the stand he took so just, that all had to acknowledge his power. He did not then, nor for many years afterward, say that the slaves ought to be immediately set free. What he did insist upon was that slavery was wrong, and that it must not be allowed to spread into territory already free; but that, gradually, in ways lawful and just to masters and slaves alike, the country should strive to get rid of it in places where it already existed. He never let his hearers lose sight of the great. underlying moral fact. "Slavery," he said, "is founded in the selfishness of man's nature; opposition to it in his love of justice." Even Senator Douglas was not prepared to admit that slavery was right. He knew that if he said that he could never be President, for the whole North would rise against him. He wished to please both sides, so he argued that it was not a question for him or for the Federal Government to decide, but one which each State and Territory must settle for itself. In answer to this plea of his that it was not a matter of morals, but of "State rights"--a mere matter of local self-government--Mr. Lincoln replied, "When the white man governs himself that is self-government; but when he governs himself and also governs another man, that is more than self government--that is despotism."

It was on these opposing grounds that the two men took their stand for the battle of argument and principle that was to continue for years, to outgrow the bounds of the State, to focus the attention of the whole country upon them, and, in the end, to have far-reaching consequences of which neither at that time dreamed. At first the field appeared much narrower, though even then the reward was a large one. Lincoln had entered the contest with no thought of political gain; but it happened that a new United States senator from Illinois had to be chosen about that time. Senators are not voted for by the people, but by the legislatures of their respective States and as a first result of all this discussion about the right or wrong of slavery it was found that the Illinois legislature, instead of having its usual large Democratic majority, was almost evenly divided. Lincoln seemed the most likely candidate; and he would have undoubtedly been chosen senator, had not five men, whose votes were absolutely necessary, stoutly refused to vote for a Whig, no matter what his views upon slavery might be. Keeping stubbornly aloof, they cast their ballots time after time for Lyman Trumbull, who was a Democrat, although as strongly opposed to slavery as Lincoln himself.

A term of six years in the United States Senate must have seemed a large prize to Lincoln just then--possibly the largest he might ever hope to gain; and it must have been a hard trial to feel it so near and then see it slipping away from him. He did what few men would have had the courage or the unselfishness to do. Putting aside all personal considerations, and intent only on making sure of an added vote against slavery in the Senate, he begged his friends to cease voting for him and to unite with those five Democrats to elect Trumbull.

"I regret my defeat moderately," he wrote to a sympathizing friend, "but I am not nervous about it." Yet it must have been particularly trying to know that with forty-five votes in his favor, and only five men standing between him and success, he had been forced to give up his own chances and help elect the very man who had defeated him.

The voters of Illinois were quick to realize the sacrifice he had made. The five stubborn men became his most devoted personal followers; and his action at this time did much to bring about a great political change in the State. All over the country old party lines were beginning to break up and re-form themselves on this one question of slavery. Keeping its old name, the Democratic party became the party in favor of slavery, while the Northern Whigs and all those Democrats who objected to slavery joined in what became known as the Republican party. It was at a great mass convention held in Bloomington in May, 1856, that the Republican party of Illinois took final shape; and it was here that Lincoln made the wonderful address which has become famous in party history as his "lost speech." There had been much enthusiasm. Favorite speakers had already made stirring addresses that had been listened to with eagerness and heartily applauded; but hardly a man moved from his seat until Lincoln should be heard. It was he who had given up the chance of being senator to help on the cause of freedom. He alone had successfully answered Douglas. Every one felt the fitness of his making the closing speech--and right nobly did he honor the demand. The spell of the hour was visibly upon him. Standing upon the platform before the members of the convention, his tall figure drawn up to its full height, his head thrown back, and his voice ringing with earnestness, he denounced the evil they had to fight in a speech whose force and power carried his hearers by storm, ending with a brilliant appeal to all who loved liberty and justice to

Come as the winds come when forests are rended; Come as the waves come when navies are stranded;

and unite with the Republican party against this great wrong.

The audience rose and answered him with cheer upon cheer. Then, after the excitement had died down, it was found that neither a full report nor even trustworthy notes of his speech had been taken. The sweep and magnetism of his oratory had carried everything before it--even the reporters had forgotten their duty, and their pencils had fallen idle. So it happened that the speech as a whole was lost. Mr. Lincoln himself could never recall what he had said; but the hundreds who heard him never forgot the scene or the lifting inspiration of his words.

Three weeks later the first national convention of the Republican party was held. John C. Fremont was nominated for President, and Lincoln received over a hundred votes for Vice-President, but fortunately, as it proved, was not selected, the honor falling to William L. Dayton of New Jersey. The Democratic candidate for President that year was James Buchanan, "a Northern man with Southern principles," very strongly in favor of slavery. Lincoln took an active part in the campaign against him, making more than fifty speeches in Illinois and the adjoining States. The Democrats triumphed, and Buchanan was elected President; but Lincoln was not discouraged, for the new Republican party had shown unexpected strength throughout the North. Indeed, Lincoln was seldom discouraged. He had an abiding faith that the people would in the long run vote wisely; and the cheerful hope he was able to inspire in his followers was always a strong point in his leadership.

In 1858, two years after this, another election took place in Illinois, on which the choice of a United States senator depended. This time it was the term of Stephen A. Douglas that was drawing to a close. He greatly desired reelection. There was but one man in the State who could hope to rival him, and with a single voice the Republicans of Illinois called upon Lincoln to oppose him. Douglas was indeed an opponent not to be despised. His friends and followers called him the "Little Giant." He was plausible, popular, quick-witted, had winning manners, was most skilful in the use of words, both to convince his hearers and, at times, to hide his real meaning. He and Lincoln were old antagonists. They had first met in the far-away Vandalia days of the Illinois legislature. In Springfield, Douglas had been the leader of the young Democrats, while Lincoln had been leader of the younger Whigs. Their rivalry had not always been confined to politics, for gossip asserted that Douglas had been one of Miss Todd's more favored suitors. Douglas in those days had no great opinion of the tall young lawyer; while Lincoln is said to have described Douglas as "the least man I ever saw"--although that referred to his rival's small stature and boyish figure, not to his mental qualities. Douglas was not only ambitious to be President: he had staked everything on the repeal of the Missouri Compromise and his statement that this question of slavery was one that every State and Territory must settle for itself, but with which the Federal Government had nothing to do. Unfortunately, his own party no longer agreed with him. Since Buchanan had become President the Democrats had advanced their ground. They now claimed that while a State might properly say whether or not it would tolerate slavery, slavery ought to be lawful in all the Territories, no matter whether their people liked it or not.

A famous law case, called the Dred Scott case, lately decided by the Supreme Court of the United States, went far toward making this really the law of the land. In its decision the court positively stated that neither Congress nor a territorial legislature had power to keep slavery out of any United States Territory. This decision placed Senator Douglas in a most curious position. It justified him in repealing the Missouri Compromise, but at the same time it absolutely denied his statement that the people of a Territory had a right to settle the slavery question to suit themselves. Being a clever juggler with words, he explained away the difference by saying that a master might have a perfect right to his slave in a Territory, and yet that right could do him no good unless it were protected by laws in force where his slave happened to be. Such laws depended entirely on the will of the people living in the Territory, and so, after all, they had the deciding voice. This reasoning brought upon him the displeasure of President Buchanan and all the Democrats who believed as he did, and Douglas found himself forced either to deny what he had already told the voters of Illinois, or to begin a quarrel with the President. He chose the latter, well knowing that to lose his reelection to the Senate at this time would end his political career. His fame as well as his quarrel with the President served to draw immense crowds to his meetings when he returned to Illinois and began speech-making, and his followers so inspired these meetings with their enthusiasm that for a time it seemed as though all real discussion would be swallowed up in noise and shouting.

Mr. Lincoln, acting on the advice of his leading friends, sent Douglas a challenge to joint debate. Douglas accepted, though not very willingly; and it was agreed that they should address the same meetings at seven towns in the State, on dates extending through August, September, and October. The terms were that one should speak an hour in opening, the other an hour and a half in reply, and the first again have half an hour to close. Douglas was to open the meeting at one place, Lincoln at the next.

It was indeed a memorable contest. Douglas, the most skilled and plausible speaker in the Democratic party, was battling for his political life. He used every art, every resource, at his command. Opposed to him was a veritable giant in stature--a man whose qualities of mind and of body were as different from those of the "Little Giant" -as could well be imagined. Lincoln was direct, forceful, logical, and filled with a purpose as lofty as his sense of right and justice was strong. He cared much for the senatorship, but he cared far more to right the wrong of slavery, and to warn people of the peril that menaced the land. Already in June he had made a speech that greatly impressed his hearers. "A house divided against itself cannot stand," he told them. "I believe this government cannot endure permanently half slave and half free. I do not expect the Union to be dissolved, I do not expect the house to fall--but I do expect it will cease to be divided. It will become all one thing or all the other"; and he went on to say that there was grave danger it might become all slave. He showed how, little by little, slavery had been gaining ground, until all it lacked now was another Supreme Court decision to make it alike lawful in all the States, North as well as South. The warning came home to the people of the North with startling force, and thereafter all eyes "were fixed upon the senatorial campaign in Illinois.

The battle continued for nearly three months. Besides the seven great joint debates, each man spoke daily, sometimes two or three times a day, at meetings of his own. Once before their audiences, Douglas's dignity as a senator afforded him no advantage, Lincoln's popularity gave him little help. Face to face with the followers of each, gathered in immense numbers and alert with jealous watchfulness, there was no escaping the rigid test of skill in argument and truth in principle. The processions and banners, the music and fireworks, of both parties were stilled and forgotten while the people listened to the three hours' battle of mind against mind.

Northern Illinois had been peopled largely from the free States, and southern Illinois from the slave States; thus the feeling about slavery in the two parts was very different. To take advantage of this, Douglas, in the very first debate, which took place at Ottawa, in northern Illinois, asked Lincoln seven questions, hoping to make him answer in a way that would be unpopular farther south. In the second debate Lincoln replied to these very frankly, and in his turn asked Douglas four questions, the second of which was whether, in Douglas's opinion, the people of any Territory could, in any lawful way, against the wish of any citizen of the United States, bar out slavery before that Territory became a State. Mr. Lincoln had long and carefully studied the meaning and effect of this question. If Douglas said, "No," he would please Buchanan and the administration Democrats, but at the cost of denying his own words. If he said, "Yes," he would make enemies of every Democrat in the South. Lincoln's friends all advised against asking the question. They felt sure that Douglas would answer, "Yes," and that this would win him his election. "If you ask it, you can never be senator," they told Lincoln. "Gentlemen," he replied, "I am killing larger game. If Douglas answers he can never be President, and the battle of 1860 is worth a hundred of this."

Both prophecies were fulfilled. Douglas answered as was expected; and though, in actual numbers, the Republicans of Illinois cast more votes than the Democrats, a legislature was chosen that rejected him to the Senate. Two years later, Lincoln, who in 1858 had not the remotest dream of such a thing, found himself the successful candidate of the Republican party for President of the United States.

To see how little Lincoln expected such an outcome it is only necessary to glance at the letters he wrote to friends at the end of his campaign against Douglas. Referring to the election to be held two years later, he said, "In that day I shall fight in the ranks, but I shall be in no one's way for any of the places." To another correspondent he expressed himself even more frankly: "Of course I wished, but I did not much expect, a better result, , , , I am glad I made the late race. It gave me a hearing on the great and durable question of the age, which I could have had in no other way; and though I now sink out of view and shall be forgotten, I believe I have made some marks which will tell for the cause of civil liberty long after I am gone."

But he was not to "sink out of view and be forgotten." Douglas himself contributed not a little toward keeping his name before the public; for shortly after their contest was ended the reelected senator started on a trip through the South to set himself right again with the Southern voters, and in every speech that he made he referred to Lincoln as the champion of "abolitionism." In this way the people were not allowed to forget the stand Lincoln had taken, and during the year 1859 they came to look upon him as the one man who could be relied on at all times to answer Douglas and Douglas's arguments.

In the autumn of that year Lincoln was asked to speak in Ohio, where Douglas was again referring to him by name. In December he was invited to address meetings in various towns in Kansas, and early in 1860 he made a speech in New York that raised him suddenly and unquestionably to the position of a national leader.

It was delivered in the hall of Cooper Institute, on the evening of February 27, 1860, before an audience of men and women remarkable for their culture, wealth and influence.

Mr. Lincoln's name and words had filled so large a space in the Eastern newspapers of late, that his listeners were very eager to see. and hear this rising Western politician. The West, even at that late day, was very imperfectly understood by the East. It was looked upon as a land of bowie-knives and pistols, of steamboat explosions, of mobs, of wild speculation and wilder adventure. What, then, would be the type, the character, the language of this speaker? How would he impress the great editor Horace Greeley, who sat among the invited guests; David Dudley Field, the great lawyer, who escorted him to the platform; William Cullen Bryant, the great poet, who presided over the meeting?

The audience quickly forgot these questioning doubts. They had but time to note Mr. Lincoln's unusual height, his rugged, strongly marked features, the clear ring of his high-pitched voice, the commanding earnestness of his manner. Then they became completely absorbed in what he was saying. He began quietly, soberly, almost as if he were arguing a case before a court. In his entire address he uttered neither an anecdote nor a jest. If any of his hearers came expecting the style or manner of the Western stump-speaker, they met novelty of an unlooked-for kind; for such was the apt choice of words, the simple strength of his reasoning, the fairness of every point he made, the force of every conclusion he drew, that his listeners followed him, spellbound. He spoke on the subject that he had so thoroughly mastered and that was now uppermost in men's minds--the right or wrong of slavery. He laid bare the complaints and demands of the Southern leaders, pointed out the injustice of their threat to break up the Union if their claims were not granted, stated forcibly the stand taken by the Republican party, and brought his speech to a close with the short and telling appeal:

"Let us have faith that right makes might, and in that faith let us, to the end, dare to do our duty as we understand it."

The attention with which it was followed, the applause that greeted its telling points, and the enthusiasm of the Republican journals next morning showed that Lincoln's Cooper Institute speech had taken New York by storm. It was printed in full in four of the leading daily papers of the city, and immediately reprinted in pamphlet form. From New York Mr. Lincoln made a tour of speech-making through several of the New England States, where he was given a hearty welcome, and listened to with an eagerness that showed a marked result at the spring elections. The interest of the working-men who heard these addresses was equaled, perhaps excelled, by the pleased surprise of college professors and men of letters when they found that the style and method of this self-taught popular Western orator would stand the test of their most searching professional criticism.

One other audience he had during this trip, if we may trust report, which, while neither as learned as the college professors, nor perhaps as critical as the factory-men, was quite as hard to please, and the winning of whose approval shows another side of this great and many-sided man. A teacher in a Sunday-school in the Five Points district of New York, at that time one of the worst parts of the city, has told how, one morning, a tall, thin, unusual-looking man entered and sat quietly listening to the exercises. His face showed such genuine interest that he was asked if he would like to speak to the children. Accepting the invitation with evident pleasure, he stepped forward and began a simple address that quickly charmed the roomful of youngsters into silence. His language was singularly beautiful, his voice musical with deep feeling. The faces of his little listeners drooped into sad earnestness at his words of warning, and brightened again when he spoke of cheerful promises. "Go on! Oh, do go on!" they begged when at last he tried to stop. As he left the room somebody asked his name. "Abraham Lincoln, from Illinois," was the courteous reply.

VI. THE NEW PRESIDENT

Lincoln's great skill and wisdom in his debate with Douglas turned the eyes of the whole country upon him; and the force and logic of his Cooper Institute speech convinced every one that in him they had discovered a new national leader. He began to be mentioned as a possible candidate for President in the election which was to take place that fall to choose a successor to President Buchanan. Indeed, quite a year earlier, an editor in Illinois had written to him asking permission to announce him as a candidate in his newspaper. At that time Lincoln had refused, thanking him for the compliment, but adding modestly: "I must in candor say that I do not think myself fit for the Presidency." About Christmas time, 1859, however, a number of his stanchest Illinois friends urged him to let them use his name, and he consented, not so much in the hope of being chosen, as of perhaps receiving the nomination for Vice-President, or at least of making a show of strength that would aid him at some future time to become senator. The man most talked about as the probable Republican candidate for President was William H. Seward, who was United States senator from New York, and had also been governor of that State.

The political unrest continued. Slavery was still the most absorbing topic, and it was upon their stand for or against slavery that all the Presidential candidates were chosen. The pretensions and demands of the Southern leaders had by this time passed into threats. They declared roundly that they would take their States out of the Union if slavery were not quickly made lawful all over the country, or in case a "Black Republican" President should be elected. The Democrats, unable to agree among themselves, split into two sections, the Northerners nominating Stephen A. Douglas for President, while delegates who had come to their National Convention from what were called the Cotton States chose John C. Breckinridge. A few men who had belonged to the old Whig party, but felt themselves unable to join the Republicans or either faction of the Democrats, met elsewhere and nominated John Bell.

This breaking up of their political enemies into three distinct camps greatly cheered the Republicans, and when their National Convention came together in Chicago on May 16, 1860, its members were filled with the most eager enthusiasm. Its meetings were held in a huge temporary wooden building called the Wigwam, so large that 10,000 people could easily assemble in it to watch the proceedings. Few conventions have shown such depth of feeling. Not only the delegates on the central platform, but even the spectators seemed impressed with the fact that they were taking part in a great historical event. The first two days were taken up in seating delegates, adopting a "platform" or statement of party principles, and in other necessary routine matters. On the third day, however, it was certain that balloting would begin, and crowds hurried to the Wigwam in a fever of curiosity. The New York men, sure that Seward would be the choice of the convention, marched there in a body, with music and banners. The friends of Lincoln arrived before them, and while not making so much noise or show, were doing good work for their favorite. The long nominating speeches of later years had not then come into fashion. "I take the liberty," simply said Mr. Evarts of New York, "to name as a candidate to be nominated by this convention for the office of President of the United States, William H. Seward," and at Mr. Seward's name a burst of applause broke forth, so long and loud that it seemed fairly to shake the great building. Mr. Judd, of Illinois, performed the same office of friendship for Mr. Lincoln, and the tremendous cheering that rose from the throats of his friends echoed and dashed itself against the sides of the Wigwam, died down, and began anew, until the noise that had been made by Seward's admirers dwindled to comparative feebleness. Again and again these contests of lungs and enthusiasm were repeated as other names were presented to the convention.

At last the voting began. Two names stood out beyond all the rest on the very first ballot--Seward's and Lincoln's. The second ballot showed that Seward had lost votes while Lincoln had gained them. The third ballot was begun in almost painful suspense, delegates and spectators keeping count upon their tally-sheets with nervous fingers. It was found that Lincoln had gained still more, and now only needed one and a half votes to receive the nomination. Suddenly the Wigwam became as still as a church. Everybody leaned forward to see who would break the spell. A man sprang upon a chair and reported a change of four votes to Lincoln. Then a teller shouted a name toward the skylight, and the boom of a cannon from the roof announced the nomination and started the cheering down the long Chicago streets; while inside delegation after delegation changed its votes to the victor in a whirlwind of hurrahs. That same afternoon the convention finished its labors by nominating Hannibal Hamlin of Maine for Vice-President, and adjourned--the delegates, speeding homeward on the night trains, realizing by the bonfires and cheering crowds at every little station that a memorable Presidential campaign was already begun.

During this campaign there were, then, four Presidential candidates in the field. In the order of strength shown at the election they were:

1. The Republican party, whose "platform," or statement of party principles, declared that slavery was wrong, and that its further spread should be prevented. Its candidates were Abraham Lincoln of Illinois for President, and Hannibal Hamlin of Maine for Vice-President.

2. The Douglas wing of the Democratic party, which declared that it did not pretend to decide whether slavery was right or wrong, and proposed to allow the people of each State and Territory to choose for themselves whether they would or would not have it. Its candidates were Stephen A. Douglas of Illinois for President, and Herschel V. Johnson of Georgia for Vice-President.

3. The Buchanan wing of the Democratic party, which declared that slavery was right, and whose policy was to extend it, and to make new slave States. Its candidates were John C. Breckinridge of Kentucky for President, and Joseph Lane of Oregon for Vice-President.

4. The Constitutional Union party, which ignored slavery in its platform, declaring that it recognized no political principles other than "the Constitution of the country, the Union of the States, and the enforcement of the laws." Its candidates were John Bell of Tennessee for President, and Edward Everett of Massachusetts for Vice-President.

In enthusiasm the Republicans quickly took the lead. "Wide Awake" clubs of young men, wearing caps and capes of glazed oilcloth to protect their clothing from the dripping oil of their torches, gathered in torchlight processions miles in length. Fence rails, supposed to have been made by Lincoln in his youth, were set up in party headquarters and trimmed with flowers and lighted tapers. Lincoln was called the "Rail-splitter Candidate," and this telling name, added to the equally telling "Honest Old Abe," by which he had long been known in Illinois, furnished country and city campaign orators with a powerful appeal to the sympathy and trust of the working-people of the United States. Men and women read in newspaper and pamphlet biographies the story of his humble beginnings: how he had risen by simple, earnest work and native genius, first to fame and leadership in his own State, and then to fame and leadership in the nation; and these titles quickly grew to be much more than mere party nicknames--to stand for a faith and trust destined to play no small part in the history of the next few years.

After the nominations were made Douglas went on a tour of speech-making through the South. Lincoln, on the contrary, stayed quietly at home in Springfield. His personal habits and surroundings varied little during the whole of this campaign summer. Naturally he gave up active law practice, leaving his office in charge of his partner, William H. Herndon. He spent the time during the usual business hours of each day in the governor's room of the State-house at Springfield, attended only by his private secretary, Mr. Nicolay. Friends and strangers alike were able to visit him freely and without ceremony, and few went away without being impressed by the sincere frankness of his manner and conversation.

All sorts of people came to see him: those from far-away States, East and West, as well as those from nearer home. Politicians came to ask him for future favors, and many whose only motives were friendliness or curiosity called to express their good wishes and take the Republican candidate by the hand.

He wrote no public letters, and he made no speeches beyond a few words of thanks and greeting to passing street parades. Even the strictly private letters in which he gave his advice on points in the campaign were not more than a dozen in number; but all through the long summer, while welcoming his throngs of visitors, listening to the tales of old settlers, making friends of strangers, and binding old friends closer by his ready sympathy, Mr. Lincoln watched political developments very closely, not merely to note the progress of his own chances, but with an anxious view to the future in case he should be elected. Beyond the ever-changing circle of friendly faces near him he saw the growing unrest and anger of the South, and doubtless felt the uncertainty of many good people in the North, who questioned the power of this untried Western man to guide the country through the coming perils.

Never over-confident of his own powers, his mind must at times have been full of misgivings; but it was only on the night of the election, November 6, 1860, when, sitting alone with the operators in the little telegraph-office at Springfield, he read the messages of Republican victory that fell from the wires until convinced of his election, that the overwhelming, almost crushing "weight of his coming duties and responsibilities fell upon him. In that hour, grappling resolutely and alone with the problem before him, he completed what was really the first act of his Presidency--the choice of his cabinet, of the men who were to aid him. People who doubted the will or the wisdom of their Rail-splitter Candidate need have had no fear. A weak man would have chosen this little band of counselors--the Secretary of State, the Secretary of the Treasury, and the half-dozen others who were to stand closest to him and to be at the head of the great departments of the government--from among his personal friends. A man uncertain of his own power would have taken care that no other man of strong nature with a great following of his own should be there to dispute his authority. Lincoln did the very opposite. He had a sincere belief in public opinion, and a deep respect for the popular will. In this case he felt that no men represented that popular will so truly as those whose names had been considered by the Republican National Convention in its choice of a candidate for President. So, instead of gathering about him his friends, he selected his most powerful rivals in the Republican party. William H. Seward, of New York, was to be his Secretary of State; Salmon P. Chase, of Ohio, his Secretary of the Treasury; Simon Cameron, of Pennsylvania, his Secretary of War; Edward Bates, of Missouri, his Attorney-General. The names of all of these men had been before the Convention. Each one had hoped to be President in his stead. For the other three members of his Cabinet he had to look elsewhere. Gideon Welles, of Connecticut, for Secretary of the Navy; Montgomery Blair, of Maryland, for Postmaster-General; and Caleb B. Smith, of Indiana, for Secretary of the Interior, were finally chosen. When people complained, as they sometimes did, that by this arrangement the cabinet consisted of four men who had been Democrats in the old days, and only three who had been Whigs, Lincoln smiled his wise, humorous smile and answered that he himself had been a Whig, and would always be there to make matters even. It is not likely that this exact list was in his mind on the night of the November election; but the principal names in it most certainly were. To some of these gentlemen he offered their appointments by letter. Others he asked to visit him in Springfield to talk the matter over. Much delay and some misunderstanding occurred before the list was finally completed: but when he sent it to the Senate, on the day after his inauguration, it was practically the one he had in his mind from the beginning.

A President is elected by popular vote early in November, but he is not inaugurated until the following fourth of March. Until the day of his inauguration, when he takes the oath of office and begins to discharge his duties, he is not only not President--he has no more power in the affairs of the Government than the humblest private citizen. It is easy to imagine the anxieties and misgivings that beset Mr. Lincoln during the four long months that lay between his election and his inauguration. True to their threats never to endure the rule of a "Black Republican" President, the Cotton States one after the other withdrew their senators and representatives from Congress, passed what they called "Ordinances of Secession," and declared themselves to be no longer a part of the United States. One after another, too, army and navy officers stationed in the Southern States gave up to the Southern leaders in this movement the forts, navy-yards, arsenals, mints, ships, and other government property under their charge. President Buchanan, in whose hands alone rested the power to punish these traitors and avenge their insults to the government he had sworn to protect and defend, showed no disposition to do so; and Lincoln, looking on with a heavy heart, was unable to interfere in any way. No matter how anxiously he might watch the developments at Washington or in the Cotton States, no matter what appeals might be made to him, no action of any kind was possible on his part.

The only bit of cheer that came to him and other Union men during this anxious season of waiting, was in the conduct of Major Robert Anderson at

Charleston Harbor, who, instead of following the example of other officers who were proving unfaithful, boldly defied the Southern "secessionists," and moving his little handful of soldiers into the harbor fort best fitted for defense, prepared to hold out against them until help could reach him from Washington.

In February the leaders of the Southern people met at Montgomery, Alabama, adopted a Constitution, and set up a government which they called the Confederate States of America, electing Jefferson Davis, of Mississippi, President, and Alexander H. Stephens, of Georgia, Vice-President. Stephens was the "little, slim pale-faced consumptive man" whose speech in Congress had won Lincoln's admiration years before. Davis had been the child who began his schooling so near to Lincoln in Kentucky. He had had a far different career. Good fortune had carried him to West Point, into the Mexican War, into the cabinet of President Franklin Pierce, and twice into the Senate. He had had money, high office, the best education his country could give him-- everything, it seemed, that had been denied to Lincoln. Now the two men were the chosen heads of two great opposing factions, one bent on destroying the government that had treated him so kindly; the other, for whom it had done so little, willing to lay down his life in its defense.

It must not be supposed that Lincoln remained idle during these four months of waiting. Besides completing his cabinet, and receiving his many visitors, he devoted himself to writing his inaugural address, withdrawing himself for some hours each day to a quiet room over the store of his brother-in-law, where he could think and write undisturbed. The newspaper correspondents who had gathered at Springfield, though alert for every item of news, and especially anxious for a sight of his inaugural address, seeing him every day as usual, got not the slightest hint of what he was doing.

Mr. Lincoln started on his journey to Washington on February 11, 1861 two days after Jefferson Davis had been elected President of the Confederate States of America. He went on a special train, accompanied by Mrs. Lincoln and their three children, his two private secretaries, and about a dozen personal friends. Mr. Seward had suggested that because of the unsettled condition of public affairs it would be better for the President-elect to come a week earlier; but Mr. Lincoln allowed himself only time comfortably to fill the engagements he had made to visit the State capitals and principal cities that lay on his way, to which he had been invited by State and town officials, regardless of party. The morning on which he left Springfield was dismal and stormy, but fully a thousand of his friends and neighbors assembled to bid him farewell. The weather seemed to add to the gloom and depression of their spirits, and the leave-taking was one of subdued anxiety, almost of solemnity. Mr. Lincoln took his stand in the waiting-room while his friends filed past him, often merely pressing his hand in silent emotion. The arrival of the rushing train broke in upon this ceremony, and the crowd closed about the car into which the President-elect and his party made their way. Just as they were starting, when the conductor had his hand upon the bell-rope, Mr. Lincoln stepped out upon the front platform and made the following brief and pathetic address. It was the last time his voice was to be heard in the city which had so long been his home:

"My Friends: No one not in my situation can appreciate my feeling of sadness at this parting. To this place and the kindness of these people I owe everything. Here I have lived a quarter of a century, and have passed from a young to an old man. Here my children have been born, and one is buried. I now leave, not knowing when or whether ever I may return, with a task before me greater than that which rested upon Washington. Without the assistance of that Divine Being who ever attended him, I cannot succeed. With that assistance I cannot fail. Trusting in Him who can go with me, and remain with you, and be everywhere for good, let us confidently hope that all will yet be well. To His care commending you, as I hope in your prayers you will commend me, I bid you an affectionate farewell."

The conductor gave the signal, the train rolled slowly out of the station, and the journey to Washington was begun. It was a remarkable progress. At almost every station, even the smallest, crowds had gathered to catch a glimpse of the face of the President-elect, or at least to see the flying train. At the larger stopping-places these crowds swelled to thousands, and in the great cities to almost unmanageable throngs. Everywhere there were calls for Mr. Lincoln, and if he showed himself; for a speech. Whenever there was time, he would go to the rear platform of the car and bow as the train moved away, or utter a few words of thanks and greeting. At the capitals of Indiana, Ohio, New York, New Jersey, and Pennsylvania, and in the cities of Cincinnati, Cleveland, Buffalo, New York, and Philadelphia, halts of one or two days were made, the time being filled with formal visits and addresses to each house of the legislature, street processions, large evening receptions, and other ceremonies.

Party foes as well as party friends made up these expectant crowds. Every eye was eager, every ear strained, to get some hint of the thoughts and purposes of the man who was to be the guide and head of the nation in the crisis that every one now knew to be upon the country, but the course and end of which the wisest could not foresee. In spite of all the cheers and the enthusiasm, there was also an under-current of anxiety for his personal safety, for the South had openly boasted that Lincoln would never live to be inaugurated President. He himself paid no heed to such warnings; but the railroad officials, and others who were responsible for his journey, had detectives on watch at different points to report any suspicious happenings. Nothing occurred to change the program already agreed upon until the party reached Philadelphia; but there Mr. Lincoln was met by Frederick W. Seward, the son of his future Secretary of State, with an important message from his father. A plot had been discovered to do violence to, and perhaps kill, the President-elect as he passed through the city of Baltimore. Mr. Seward and General Scott, the venerable hero of the Mexican War, who was now at the head of the army, begged him to run no risk, but to alter his plans so that a portion of his party might pass through Baltimore by a night train without previous notice. The seriousness of the warning was doubled by the fact that Mr. Lincoln had just been told of a similar, if not exactly the same, danger, by a Chicago detective employed in Baltimore by one of the great railroad companies. Two such warnings, coming from entirely different sources, could not be disregarded; for however much Mr. Lincoln might dislike to change his plans for so shadowy a danger, his duty to the people who had elected him forbade his running any unnecessary risk. Accordingly, after fulfilling all his engagements in Philadelphia and Harrisburg on February 22, he and a single companion took a night train, passed quietly through Baltimore, and arrived in Washington about daylight on the morning of February 23. This action called forth much talk, ranging from the highest praise to ridicule and blame. A reckless newspaper reporter telegraphed all over the country the absurd story that he had traveled disguised in a Scotch cap and a long military cloak. There was, of course, not a word of truth in the absurd tale. The rest of the party followed Mr. Lincoln at the time originally planned. They saw great crowds in the streets of Baltimore, but there was now no occasion for violence.

In the week that passed between his arrival and the day of his inauguration Mr. Lincoln exchanged the customary visits of ceremony with President Buchanan, his cabinet, the Supreme Court, the two houses of Congress, and other dignitaries.

Careful preparations for the inauguration had been made under the personal direction of General Scott, who held the small military force in the city ready instantly to suppress any attempt to disturb the peace and quiet of the day.

On the morning of the fourth of March President Buchanan and Citizen Lincoln, the outgoing and incoming heads of the government, rode side by side in a carriage from the Executive Mansion, or White House, as it is more commonly called, to the Capitol, escorted by an imposing procession; and at noon a great throng of people heard Mr. Lincoln read his inaugural address as he stood on the east portico of the Capitol, surrounded by all the high officials of the government. Senator Douglas, his unsuccessful rival, standing not an arm's length away from him, courteously held his hat during the ceremony. A cheer greeted him as he finished his address. Then the Chief Justice arose, the clerk opened his Bible, and Mr. Lincoln, laying his hand upon the book, pronounced the oath:

"I, Abraham Lincoln, do solemnly swear that I will faithfully execute the office of President of the United States, and will, to the best of my ability, preserve, protect, and defend the Constitution of the United States."

Amid the thundering of cannon and the applause of all the spectators, President Lincoln and Citizen Buchanan again entered their carriage and drove back from the Capitol to the Executive Mansion, on the threshold of which Mr. Buchanan, warmly shaking the hand of his successor, expressed his wishes for the personal happiness of the new President, and for the national peace and prosperity.

VII. LINCOLN AND THE WAR

It is one thing to be elected President of the United States,-- that means triumph, honor, power: it is quite another thing to perform the duties of President,--for that means labor, disappointment, difficulty, even danger. Many a man envied Abraham Lincoln when, in the stately pomp of inauguration and with the plaudits of the spectators ringing about him, he took the oath of office which for four years transforms an American citizen into the ruler of these United States. Such envy would have been changed to deepest sympathy if they could have known what lay before him. After the music and cannon were dumb, after the flags were all furled and the cheering crowds had vanished, the shadows of war fell about the Executive Mansion, and its new occupant remained face to face with his heavy task--a task which, as he had truly said in his speech at Springfield, was greater than that which rested upon Washington.

Then, as never before, he must have realized the peril of the nation, with its credit gone, its laws defied, its flag insulted. The South had carried out its threat, and seven million Americans were in revolt against the idea that "all men are created equal," while twenty million other Americans were bent upon defending that idea. For the moment both sides had paused to see how the new President would treat this attempt at secession. It must be constantly borne in mind that the rebellion in the Southern States with which Mr. Lincoln had to deal was not a sudden revolution, but a conspiracy of slow growth and long planning. As one of its actors frankly admitted, it was "not an event of a day. It is not anything produced by Mr. Lincoln's election. . . . It is a matter which has been gathering head for thirty years." Its main object, it must also be remembered, was the spread of slavery. Alexander H. Stephens, in a speech made shortly after he became the Confederate Vice-President, openly proclaimed slavery to be the "corner-stone" of the new government. For years it had been the dream of southern leaders to make the Ohio River the northern boundary of a great slave empire, with everything lying to the south of that, even the countries of South and Central America, as parts of their system. Though this dream was never to be realized, the Confederacy finally came to number eleven States (Alabama, Mississippi, Louisiana, South Carolina, North Carolina, Florida, Texas, Arkansas, Tennessee, Virginia and Georgia), and to cover a territory of more than 750,000 square miles--larger than England, Scotland, Ireland, France, Spain, Germany and Switzerland put together, with a coast line 3,500 miles long, and a land frontier of over 7,000 miles.

President Buchanan's timidity and want of spirit had alone made this great rebellion possible, for although it had been "gathering head for thirty years" it was only within the last few months that it had come to acts of open treason and rebellion. President Buchanan had opportunity and ample power to crush it when the conspirators first began to show their hands. Instead he wavered, and delayed, while they grew bold under his lack of decision, imagining that they would have a bloodless victory, and even boasting that they would take Washington for their capital; or, if the new President should thwart them and make them fight, that they would capture Philadelphia and dictate the peace they wanted from Independence Hall.

By the time Mr. Lincoln came into office the conspiracy had grown beyond control by any means then in the hands of a President, though men on both sides still vainly hoped that the troubles of the country might be settled without fighting. Mr. Lincoln especially wished to make very sure that if it ever came to a matter of war, the fault should not lie with the North.

In his inaugural address he had told the South that he would use the power confided to him to hold and occupy the places belonging to the Government, and to collect the taxes; but beyond what might be necessary for these objects, he would not use force among the people anywhere. His peaceful policy was already harder to follow than he realized. Before he had been President twenty-four hours word came from Major Anderson, still defying the conspirators from Fort Sumter in Charleston Harbor, that his little garrison was short of food, and must speedily surrender unless help reached them. The rebels had for weeks been building batteries to attack the fort, and with Anderson's report came the written opinions of his officers that it would require an army of 20,000 men to relieve it. They might as well have asked for twenty thousand archangels, for at that time the entire army of the United States numbered but 17,113 men, and these were doing duty, not only in the Southern and Eastern States, but were protecting settlers from Indians on the great western frontier, and guarding the long Canadian and Mexican boundaries as well. Yet Anderson and his men could not be left to their fate without even an attempt to help them, though some of the high military and naval officers hastily called into council by the new President advised this course. It was finally decided to notify the Confederates that a ship carrying food, but no soldiers, would be sent to his relief. If they chose to fire upon that it would be plainly the South, and not the North, that began the war.

Days went on, and by the middle of April the Confederate government found itself forced to a fatal choice. Either it must begin war, or allow the rebellion to collapse. All its claims to independence were denied; the commissioner it sent to Washington on the pretense that they were agents of a foreign country were politely refused a hearing, yet not one angry word, or provoking threat, or a single harmful act had come from the "Black Republican" President. In his inaugural he had promised the people of the South peace and protection, and offered them the benefit of the mails. Even now, all he proposed to do was to send bread to Anderson and his hungry soldiers. His prudent policy placed them where, as he had told them, they could have no war unless they themselves chose to begin it.

They did choose to begin it. The rebellion was the work of ambitious men, who had no mind to stop at that late day and see their labor go for nothing. The officer in charge of their batteries was ordered to open fire on Fort Sumter if

Anderson refused to surrender; and in the dim light of dawn on April 12, 1861, just as the outline of Fort Sumter began to show itself against a brightening sky, the shot that opened the Civil War rose from a rebel battery and made its slow and graceful curve upon Sumter. Soon all the batteries were in action, and the fort was replying with a will. Anderson held out for a day and a half, until his cartridges were all used up, his flagstaff had been shot away, and the wooden buildings inside the fort were on fire. Then, as the ships with supplies had not yet arrived, and he had neither food nor ammunition, he was forced to surrender.

The news of the firing upon Fort Sumter changed the mood of the country as if by magic. By deliberate act of the Confederate government its attempt at peaceable secession had been changed to active war. The Confederates gained Fort Sumter, but in doing so they roused the patriotism of the North to a firm resolve that this insult to the flag should be redressed, and that the unrighteous experiment of a rival government founded upon slavery as its "cornerstone," should never succeed. In one of his speeches on the journey to Washington Mr. Lincoln had said that devoted as he was to peace, it might become necessary to "put the foot down firmly." That time had now come. On April 15, the day after the fall of Fort Sumter, all the newspapers of the country printed the President's call to arms, ordering out 75,000 militia for three months, and directing Congress to meet in special session on July 4, 1861. The North rallied instantly to the support of the Government, and offered him twice the number of soldiers he asked for.

Nothing more clearly shows the difference between President Lincoln and President Buchanan than the way in which the two men met the acts of the Southern Rebellion. President Buchanan temporized and delayed when he had plenty of power. President Lincoln, without a moment's hesitation accepted the great and unusual responsibility thrust upon him, and at once issued orders for buying ships, moving troops, advancing money to Committees of Safety, and for other military and naval measures for which at the moment he had no express authority from Congress. As soon as Congress came together on July 4, he sent a message explaining his action, saying: "It became necessary for me to choose whether, using only the existing means . . . . which Congress had provided, I should let the Government fall at once into ruin, or whether availing myself of the broader powers conferred by the Constitution in cases of insurrection, I would make an effort to save it with all its blessings for the present age and for posterity." Congress, it is needless to say, not only approved all that he had done, but gave him practically unlimited powers for dealing with the rebellion in future.

It soon became evident that no matter how ready and willing to fight for their country the 75,000 volunteers might be, they could not hope to put down the rebellion, because the time for which they had enlisted would be almost over before they could receive the training necessary to change them from valiant citizens into good soldiers. Another call was therefore issued, this time for men to serve three years or during the war, and also for a large number of sailors to man the new ships that the Government was straining every nerve to buy, build and otherwise make ready.

More important, however, than soldiers trained or untrained, was the united will of the people of the North; and most important of all the steadfast and courageous soul of the man called to direct the struggle. Abraham Lincoln, the poor frontier boy, the struggling young lawyer, the Illinois politician, whom many, even among the Republicans who voted to elect him President, thought scarcely fit to hold a much smaller office, proved beyond question the man for the task gifted above all his associates with wisdom and strength to meet the great emergencies as they arose during the four years' war that had already begun.

Since this is the story of Mr. Lincoln's life, and not of the Civil War, we cannot attempt to follow the history of the long contest as it unfolded itself day by day and month by month, or even to stop to recount a list of the great battles that drenched the land in blood. It was a mighty struggle, fought by men of the same race and kindred, often by brother against brother. Each fought for what he felt to be right; and their common inheritance of courage and iron will, of endurance and splendid bravery and stubborn pluck, made this battle of brothers the more bitter as it was the more prolonged. It ranged over an immense extent of country; but because Washington was the capital of the Union, and Richmond, Virginia, the capital of the Confederacy, and the desire of each side was to capture the chief city of the other, the principal fighting ground, during the whole war, lay between these two towns, with the Alleghany Mountains on the west, and Chesapeake Bay on the east. Between the Alleghanies and the Mississippi River another field of warfare developed itself, on which some of the hardest battles were fought, and the greatest victories won. Beyond the Mississippi again stretched another great field, bounded only by the Rocky Mountains and the Rio Grande. But the principal fighting in this field was near or even on the Mississippi, in the efforts made by both Unionists and Confederates to keep and hold the great highway of the river, so necessary for trade in time of peace, and for moving armies in time of war.

On this immense battle-ground was fought one of the most costly wars of modern times, with soldiers numbering a million men on each side; in which, counting battles and skirmishes small and great, an average of two engagements a day were fought for four long years, two millions of money were used up every twenty-four hours, and during which the unholy prize of slavery, for which the Confederate States did battle, was completely swept away.

Though the tide of battle ebbed and flowed, defeat and victory may be said to have been nearly evenly divided. Generally speaking, success was more often on the side of the South during the first half of the war; with the North, during the latter half. The armies were equally brave; the North had the greater territory from which to draw supplies; and the end came, not when one side had beaten the other, man for man, but when the South had been drained of fighting men and food and guns, and slavery had perished in the stress of war.

Fortunately for all, nobody at the beginning dreamed of the length of the struggle. Even Lincoln's stout heart would have been dismayed if he could have foreseen all that lay before him. The task that he could see was hard and perplexing enough. Everything in Washington was in confusion. No President ever had such an increase of official work as Lincoln during the early months of his administration. The halls and ante-rooms of the Executive Mansion were literally crowded with people seeking appointment to office; and the new appointments that were absolutely necessary were not half finished when the firing on Fort Sumter began active war. This added to the difficulty of sifting the loyal from the disloyal, and the yet more pressing labor of organizing an immense new army.

Hundreds of clerks employed in the Government Departments left their desks and hurried South, crippling the service just at the time when the sudden increase of work made their presence doubly needed. A large proportion of the officers of the Army and Navy, perhaps as many as one-third, gave their skill and services to the Confederacy, feeling that their allegiance was due to their State or section rather than to the general government. Prominent among these was Robert E. Lee, who had been made a colonel by Lincoln, and whom General Scott had recommended as the most promising officer to command the new force of 75,000 men called out by the President's proclamation. He chose instead to resign and cast his fortunes with the South, where he became the head of all the Confederate armies. The loss to the Union and gain to the Confederate cause by his action is hard to measure, since in him the Southern armies found a commander whose surpassing courage and skill inspired its soldiers long after all hope of success was gone. Cases such as this gave the President more anxiety than all else. It seemed impossible to know whom to trust. An officer might come to him in the morning protesting devotion to the Union, and by night be gone to the South. Mr. Lincoln used to say at this time that he felt like a man letting rooms at one end of his house while the other end was on fire.

The situation grew steadily worse. Maryland refused to allow United States soldiers to cross her territory, and the first attempt to bring troops through Baltimore from the North ended in a bloody riot, and the burning of railroad bridges to prevent help from reaching Washington. For three days Washington was entirely cut off from the North, either by telegraph or mail. General Scott hastily prepared the city for a siege, taking possession of all the large supplies of flour and provisions in town, and causing the Capitol and other public buildings to be barricaded. Though President Lincoln did not doubt the final arrival of help, he, like everyone else, was very anxious, and found it hard to understand the long delay. He knew that troops had started from the North. Why did they not arrive? They might not be able to go through Baltimore, but they could certainly go around it. The distance was not great. What if twenty miles of railroad had been destroyed, were the soldiers unable to march? Always calm and self-controlled, he gave no sign in the presence of others of the anxiety that weighed so heavily upon him. Very likely the visitors who saw him during those days thought that he hardly realized the plight of the city; yet an inmate of the White House, passing through the President's office when the day's work was done and he imagined himself alone, saw him pause in his absorbed walk up and down the floor, and gaze long out of the window in the direction from which the troops were expected to appear. Then, unconscious of any hearer, and as if the words were wrung from him by anguish, he exclaimed, "Why don't they come, why don't they come

The New York Seventh Regiment was the first to "come." By a roundabout route it reached Washington on the morning of April 25, and, weary and travel-worn, but with banners flying and music playing, marched up Pennsylvania Avenue to the big white Executive Mansion, bringing cheer to the President and renewed courage to those timid citizens whose fright during this time had almost paralyzed the life of the town. Taking renewed courage they once more opened their houses and the shops that had been closed since the beginning of the blockade, and business began anew.

The greater part of the three months' regiments had been ordered to Washington, and the outskirts of the capital soon became a busy military camp. The great Departments of the Government, especially of War and Navy, could not immediately handle the details of all this sudden increase of work. Men were volunteering rapidly enough, but there was sore need of rations to feed them, money to pay them, tents to shelter them, uniforms to clothe them, rifles to arm them, officers to drill them, and of transportation to carry them to the camps of instruction where they must receive their training and await further orders. In this carnival of patriotism and hurly-burly of organization the weaknesses as well as the virtues of human nature quickly showed themselves; and, as if the new President had not already enough to distress and harass his mind, almost every case of confusion and delay was brought to him for complaint and correction. On him also fell the delicate and serious task of deciding hundreds of novel questions as to what he and his cabinet ministers had and had not the right to do under the Constitution.

The month of May slipped away in all these preparatory vexations; but the great machine of war, once started, moved on as it always does, from arming to massing of troops, and from that to skirmish and battle. In June small fights began to occur between the Union and Confederate armies. The first large battle of the war took place at Bull Run, about thirty-two miles southwest of Washington, on July 21, 1861. It ended in a victory for the Confederates, though their army was so badly crippled by. its losses that it made no further forward movement during the whole of the next autumn and winter.

The shock of this defeat was deep and painful to the people of the North, not yet schooled to patience, or to the uncertainties of war. For weeks the newspapers, confident of success, had been clamoring for action, and the cry, "Forward to Richmond," had been heard on every hand. At first the people would not believe the story of a defeat; but it was only too true. By night the beaten Union troops were pouring into the fortifications around Washington, and the next day a horde of stragglers found their way across the bridges of the Potomac into the city.

President Lincoln received the news quietly, as was his habit, without any visible sign of distress or alarm, but he remained awake and in his office all that Sunday night, listening to the excited tales of congressmen and senators who, with undue curiosity, had followed the army and witnessed some of the sights and sounds of battle; and by dawn on Monday he had practically made up his mind as to the probable result and what he must do in consequence.

The loss of the battle of Bull Run was a bitter disappointment to him. He saw that the North was not to have the easy victory it anticipated; and to him personally it brought a great and added care that never left him during the war. Up to that time the North had stood by him as one man in its eager resolve to put down the rebellion. From this time on, though quite as determined, there was division and disagreement among the people as to how this could best be done. Parties formed themselves for or against this or that general, or in favor of this or that method and no other of carrying on the war. In other words, the President and his "administration"--the cabinet and other officers under him-- became, from this time on, the target of criticism for all the failures of the Union armies, and for all the accidents and mistakes and unforeseen delays of war. The self-control that Mr. Lincoln had learned in the hard school of his boyhood, and practised during all the long struggle of his young manhood, had been severe and bitter training, but nothing else could have prepared him for the great disappointments and trials of the crowning years of his life. He had learned to endure patiently, to reason calmly, never to be unduly sure of his own opinion; but, having taken counsel of the best advice at his command, to continue in the path that he felt to be right, regardless of criticism or unjust abuse. He had daily and hourly to do all this. He was strong and courageous, with a steadfast belief that the right would triumph in the end; but his nature was at the same time sensitive and tender, and the sorrows and pain of others hurt him more than did his own.

VIII. UNSUCCESSFUL GENERALS

So far Mr. Lincoln's new duties as President had not placed him at any disadvantage with the members of his cabinet. On the old question of slavery he was as well informed and had clearer ideas than they. On the new military questions that had come up since the inauguration, they, like himself, had to rely on the advice of experienced officers of the army and navy; and since these differed greatly, Mr. Lincoln's powerful mind was as able to reach true conclusions as were men who had been governors and senators. Yet the idea lingered that because he had never before held high office, and because a large part of his life had been passed in the rude surroundings of the frontier, he must of necessity be lacking in power to govern--be weaker in will, without tact or culture--must in every way be less fitted to cope with the difficult problems so rapidly coming upon the administration.

At the beginning even Secretary Seward shared this view. Mr. Lincoln must have been surprised indeed, when, on the first day of April, exactly four weeks after his inauguration, his Secretary of State, the man he justly looked upon as the chief member of his cabinet, handed him a paper on which were written "Some Thoughts for the President's Consideration." It was most grave and dignified in language, but in substance bluntly told Mr. Lincoln that after a month's trial the Administration was without a policy, domestic or foreign, and that this must be remedied at once. It advised shifting the issue at home from slavery to the question of Union or disunion; and counseled the adoption of an attitude toward Europe which could not have failed to rouse the anger of the principal foreign nations. It added that the President or some member of his cabinet must make it his constant duty to pursue and direct whatever policy should be adopted, and hinted very plainly that although he, Mr. Seward, did not seek such responsibility, he was willing to assume it. The interest of this remarkable paper for us lies in the way Mr. Lincoln treated it, and the measure that treatment gives us of his generosity and self-control. An envious or a resentful man could not have wished a better opportunity to put a rival under his feet; but though Mr. Lincoln doubtless thought the incident very strange, it did not for a moment disturb his serenity or his kindly judgment. He answered in a few quiet sentences that showed no trace of passion or even of excitement; and on the central suggestion that some one person must direct the affairs of the government, replied with dignity "if this must be done, I must do it," adding that on affairs of importance he desired and supposed he had a right to have the advice of all the members of his cabinet. This reply ended the matter, and as far as is known, neither of them ever mentioned the subject again. Mr. Lincoln put the papers away in an envelope, and no word of the affair came to the public until years after both men were dead. In one mind at least there was no longer a doubt that the cabinet had a master. Mr. Seward recognized the President's kindly forbearance, and repaid it by devotion and personal friendship until the day of his tragic death.

If, after this experience, the Secretary of State needed any further proof of Mr. Lincoln's ability to rule, it soon came to him, for during the first months of the war matters abroad claimed the attention of the cabinet, and with these also the untried western man showed himself better fitted to deal than his more experienced advisers. Many of the countries of Europe, especially France and England, wished the South to succeed. France because of plans that Emperor Napoleon III had for founding French colonies on American soil, and England because such success would give her free cotton for her mills and factories. England became so friendly toward the rebels that Mr. Seward, much irritated, wrote a despatch on May 21, 1861, to Charles Francis Adams, the American Minister at London, which, if it had been sent as he wrote it, would almost certainly have brought on war between the two countries. It set forth justly and with courage what the United States government would and would not endure from foreign powers during the war with the South, but it had been penned in a heat of indignation, and was so blunt and exasperating as to suggest intentional disrespect. When Mr. Seward read it to the President the latter at once saw this, and taking it from his Secretary of State kept it by him for further consideration. A second reading showed him that his first impression was correct. Thereupon the frontier lawyer, taking his pen, went carefully over the whole dispatch, and by his corrections so changed the work of the trained and experienced statesman as entirely to remove its offensive tone, without in the least altering its force or courage.

Once again during 1861 the country was in serious danger of war with England, and the action of President Lincoln at this time proved not only that he had the will to be just, even when his own people were against him, but had the skill to gain real advantage from what seemed very like defeat. One of the earliest and most serious tasks of the Government had been to blockade the southern ports, in order to prevent supplies from foreign countries reaching the southern people, especially the southern armies. Considering the great length of coast to be patrolled, and the small size of the navy at the commencement of the struggle, this was done with wonderful quickness, and proved in the main effective, though occasionally a rebel boat managed to slip in or out without being discovered and fired upon by the ships on guard.

In November Captain Charles Wilkes learned that Ex-Senators J. M. Mason and John Slidell, two prominent Confederates bound on an important mission to Europe, had succeeded in reaching Cuba, and from there had taken passage for England on the British mail steamer Trent. He stopped the Trent and took Mason and Slidell prisoners, afterward allowing the steamer to proceed on her way. The affair caused intense excitement both in England and in the United States, and England began instant preparations for war. Lord Lyons, the British Minister at Washington, was instructed to demand the release of the prisoners and a suitable apology within one week, and if this were refused, to close his legation and come home. It was fortunate that Lord Lyons and Mr. Seward were close personal friends, and could, in spite of the excitement of both countries, discuss the matter calmly and without anger. Their conferences were brought to an end by Mr. Lincoln's decision to give up the prisoners. In the North their capture had been greeted with extravagant joy. Newspapers rang with praises of Captain Wilkes; his act was officially approved by the Secretary of the Navy, and the House of Representatives passed a resolution thanking him for his "brave, adroit, and patriotic conduct." In the face of all this it must have been hard indeed for Mr. Lincoln to order that Mason and Slidell be given up; but though he shared the first impulse of rejoicing, he soon became convinced that this must be done. War with England must certainly be avoided; and Captain Wilkes, by allowing the Trent to proceed on her voyage, instead of bringing her into port with the prisoners, had put it out of the power of his Government to prove, under international law, that the capture was justified. Besides all else, the President's quick mind saw, what others failed to note, that by giving up the prisoners as England demanded, the United States would really gain an important diplomatic victory. For many years England had claimed the right to stop and search vessels at sea when she had reason to believe they carried men or goods hostile to her interests. The United States denied the right, and yet this was exactly what Captain Wilkes had done in stopping the Trent. By giving up the prisoners the United States would thus force England to admit that her own claim had been unjust, and bind her in future to respect the rights of other ships at sea. Excited American feeling was grievously disappointed, and harsh criticism of the Administration for thus yielding to a foreign country was not wanting; but American good sense soon saw the justice of the point taken and the wisdom of Mr. Lincoln's course.

"He that is slow to anger," says the proverb, "is better than the mighty, and he that ruleth his spirit than he that taketh a city." Great as was his self-control in other matters, nowhere did Mr. Lincoln's slowness to anger and nobility of spirit show itself more than in his dealings with the generals of the Civil War. He had been elected President. Congress had given him power far exceeding that which any President had ever exercised before. As President he was also Commander-in-Chief of the Army and Navy of the United States. By proclamation he could call forth great armies and he could order those armies to go wherever he chose to send them; but even he had no power to make generals with the genius and the training necessary to lead them instantly to success. He had to work with the materials at hand, and one by one he tried the men who seemed best fitted for the task, giving each his fullest trust and every aid in his power. They were as eager for victory and as earnest of purpose as himself, but in every case some misfortune or some fault marred the result, until the country grew weary with waiting; discouragement overshadowed hope, and misgiving almost engulfed his own strong soul. Then, at last, the right men were found, the battles were all fought, and the war was at an end.

His kindness and patience in dealing with the generals who did not succeed is the wonder of all who study the history of the Civil War. The letters he wrote to them show better than whole volumes of description could do the helpful and forbearing spirit in which he sought to aid them. First among these unsuccessful generals was George B. McClellan, who had been called to Washington after the battle of Bull Run and placed in charge of the great new army of three years' volunteers that was pouring so rapidly into the city. McClellan proved a wonderful organizer. Under his skilful direction the raw recruits went to their camps of instruction, fell without confusion or delay into brigades and divisions, were supplied with equipments, horses and batteries, and put through a routine of drill, tactics and reviews that soon made this Army of the Potomac, as it was called, one of the best prepared armies the world has ever seen--a perfect fighting machine of over 150,000 men and more than 200 guns. General McClellan excelled in getting soldiers ready to fight, but he did not succeed in leading them to fruitful victory. At first the administration had great hopes of him as a commander. He was young, enthusiastic, winning, and on arriving in Washington seemed amazed and deeply touched by the confidence reposed in him. "I find myself," he wrote to his wife, "in a new and strange position here, President, cabinet, General Scott, and all, deferring to me. By some strange operation of magic I seem to have become the power of the land." His rise in military rank had equaled the inventions of fairy tales. He had been only a captain during the Mexican war. Then he resigned. Two months after volunteering for the Civil War he found himself a Major General in the Regular Army. For a short time his zeal and activity seemed to justify this amazing good fortune. In a fortnight however he began to look upon himself as the principal savior of his country. He entered upon a quarrel with General Scott which soon drove that old hero into retirement and out of his pathway. He looked upon the cabinet as a set of "geese," and seeing that the President was kind and unassuming in discussing military affairs, he formed the habit of expressing contempt for him in letters to confidential friends. This feeling grew until it soon reached a mark of open disrespect, but the President's conduct toward him did not change. Mr. Lincoln's nature was too forgiving, and the responsibility that lay upon him was too heavy for personal resentment. For fifteen months he strove to make McClellan succeed even in spite of himself. He gave him help, encouragement, the most timely suggestions. He answered his ever-increasing complaints with unfailing self-control. It was not that he did not see McClellan's faults. He saw them, and felt them keenly. "If Gen. McClellan does not want to use the army, I would like to borrow it," he said one day, stung by the General's inactivity into a sarcasm he seldom allowed himself to use. But his patience was not exhausted. McClellan had always more soldiers than the enemy, at Antietam nearly double his numbers, yet his constant cry was for re-enforcements. Regiments were sent him that could ill be spared from other points. Even when his fault-finding reached the height of telegraphing to the Secretary of War, "If I save this army now I tell you plainly that I owe no thanks to you or to any other persons in Washington. You have done your best to sacrifice this army," the President answered him kindly and gently, without a sign of resentment, anxious only to do everything in his power to help on the cause of the war. It was of no avail. Even the great luck of finding a copy of General Lee's orders and knowing exactly what his enemy meant to do, at a time when the Confederate general had only about half as many troops as he had, and these were divided besides, did not help him to success. All he could do even then was to fight the drawn battle of Antietam, and allow Lee to get away safely across the Potomac River into Virginia. After this the President's long-suffering patience was at an end, but he did not remove McClellan until he had visited the Army of the Potomac in person. What he saw on that visit assured him that it could never succeed under such a general. "Do you know what that is ?" he asked a friend, waving his arm towards the white tents of the great army. "It is the Army of the Potomac, I suppose," was the wondering answer. "So it is called," replied the President, in a tone of suppressed indignation. "But that is a mistake. It is only McClellan's bodyguard." On November 5, 1862, McClellan was relieved from command, and this ended his military career.

There were others almost equally trying. There was General Fremont, who had been the Republican candidate for President in 1856. At the beginning of the war he was given a command at St. Louis and charged with the important duty of organizing the military strength of the northwest, holding the State of Missouri true to the Union, and leading an expedition down the Mississippi River. Instead of accomplishing all that had been hoped for, his pride of opinion and unwillingness to accept help or take advice from those about him, caused serious embarrassment and made unending trouble. The President's kindness and gentleness in dealing with his faults were as marked as they were useless.

There was the long line of commanders who one after the other tried and failed in the tasks allotted to them, while the country waited and lost courage, and even Mr. Lincoln's heart sank. His care and wisdom and sorrow dominated the whole long persistent struggle. That first sleepless night of his after the battle of Bull Run was but the beginning of many nights and days through which he kept unceasing watch. From the time in June, 1861, when he had been called upon to preside over the council of war that decided upon the Bull Run campaign, he devoted every spare moment to the study of such books upon the art of war as would aid him in solving the questions that he must face as Commander-in-Chief of the armies. With his quick mind and unusual power of logic he made rapid progress in learning the fixed and accepted rules on which all military writers agree. His mastery of the difficult science became so thorough, and his understanding of military situations so clear, that he has been called, by persons well fitted to judge, "the ablest strategist of the war." Yet he never thrust his knowledge upon his generals. He recognized that it was their duty, not his, to fight the battles, and since this was so, they ought to be allowed to fight them in their own way. He followed their movements with keenest interest and with a most astonishing amount of knowledge, giving a hint here, and a suggestion there, when he felt that he properly could, but he rarely gave a positive order.

There is not space to quote the many letters in which he showed his military wisdom, or his kindly interest in the welfare and success of the different generals. One of the most remarkable must however be quoted. It is the letter he wrote to General Joseph Hooker on placing him in command of the Army of the Potomac in January, 1863, after McClellan's many failures had been followed by the crushing defeat of the army under General McClellan's successor, General Burnside, at the battle of Fredericksburg, on December 13, 1862.

"I have placed you," he wrote on giving General Hooker the command, "at the head of the Army of the Potomac. Of course I have done this upon what appear to me to be sufficient reasons, and yet I think it best for you to know that there are some things in regard to which I am not quite satisfied with you. I believe you to be a brave and skilful soldier, which, of course, I like. I also believe you do not mix politics with your profession, in which you are right. You have confidence in yourself, which is a valuable, if not an indispensable quality. You are ambitious, which, within reasonable bounds, does good rather than harm; but I think that during General Burnside's command of the army you have taken council of your ambition and thwarted him as much as you could, in which you did a great wrong to the country, and to a most meritorious and honorable brother officer. I have heard, in such a way as to believe it, of your recently saying that both the army and the Government needed a dictator. Of course it was not for this, but in spite of it, that I have given you the command. Only those generals who gain successes can set up dictators. What I now ask of you is military success, and I will risk the dictatorship. The government will support you to the utmost of its ability, which is neither more nor less than it has done and will do for all commanders. I much fear that the spirit which you have aided to infuse into the army, of criticising their commander and withholding confidence from him, will now turn upon you. I shall assist you as far as I can, to put it down. Neither you nor Napoleon, if he were alive again, could get any good out of an army while such a spirit prevails in it. And now, beware of rashness. Beware of rashness, but with energy and sleepless vigilance go forward and give us victories."

Perhaps no other piece of his writing shows as this does how completely the genius of the President rose to the full height of his duties and responsibilities. From beginning to end it speaks the language and breathes the spirit of the great ruler, secure in popular confidence and in official authority.

Though so many of the great battles during the first half of the war were won by the Confederates, military successes came to the North of course from time to time. With such fine armies and such earnest generals the tide of battle could not be all one way; and even when the generals made mistakes, the heroic fighting and endurance of the soldiers and under-officers gathered honor out of defeat, and shed the luster of renown over results of barren failure. But it was a weary time, and the outlook was very dark. The President never despaired. On the most dismal day of the whole dismal summer of 1862 he sent Secretary Seward to New York with a confidential letter full of courage, to be shown such of the governors of free States as could be hastily summoned to meet him there. In it he said: "I expect to maintain this contest until successful, or till I die, or am conquered, or my term expires, or Congress or the country forsake me," and he asked for 100,000 fresh volunteers with which to carry on the war. His confidence was not misplaced. The governors of eighteen free States offered him three times the number, and still other calls for troops followed. Soon a popular song, "We are coming, Father Abraham, three hundred thousand strong," showed the faith and trust of the people in the man at the head of the Government, and how cheerfully they met the great calls upon their patriotism.

So, week after week and month after month, he faced the future, never betraying a fear that the Union would not triumph in the end, but grieving sorely at the long delay. Many who were not so sure came to him with their troubles. He was beset by night and by day by people who had advice to give or complaints to make. They besought him to dismiss this or that General, to order such and such a military movement; to do a hundred things that he, in his great wisdom, felt were not right, or for which the time had not yet come. Above all, he was implored to take some decided and far-reaching action upon slavery.

IX. FREEDOM FOR THE SLAVES

By no means the least of the evils of slavery was a dread which had haunted every southern household from the beginning of the government that the slaves might one day rise in revolt and take sudden vengeance upon their masters. This vague terror was greatly increased by the outbreak of the Civil War. It stands to the lasting credit of the negro race that the wrongs of their long bondage provoked them to no such crime, and that the war seems not to have suggested, much less started any such attempt. Indeed, even when urged to violence by white leaders, as the slaves of Maryland had been in 1859 during John Browns s raid at Harper's Ferry, they had refused to respond. Nevertheless it was plain from the first that slavery was to play an important part in the Civil War. Not only were the people of the South battling for the principle of slavery; their slaves were a great source of military strength. They were used by the Confederates in building forts, hauling supplies, and in a hundred ways that added to the effectiveness of their armies in the field. On the other hand the very first result of the war was to give adventurous or discontented slaves a chance to escape into Union camps, where, even against orders to the contrary, they found protection for the sake of the help they could give as cooks, servants, or teamsters, the information they brought about the movements of the enemy, or the great service they were able to render as guides. Practically therefore, at the very start, the war created a bond of mutual sympathy between the southern negro and the Union volunteer; and as fast as Union troops advanced and secession masters fled, a certain number found freedom in Union camps.

At some points this became a position of embarrassment to Union commanders. A few days after General Butler took command of the Union troops at Fortress Monroe in May, 1861, the agent of a rebel master came to insist on the return of three slaves, demanding them under the fugitive-slave law. Butler replied that since their master claimed Virginia to be a foreign country and no longer a part of the United States, he could not at the same time claim that the fugitive slave law was in force, and that his slaves would not be given up unless he returned and took the oath of allegiance to the United States. In reporting this, a newspaper pointed out that as the breastworks and batteries which had risen so rapidly for Confederate defense were built by slave labor, negroes were undoubtedly "contraband of war," like powder and shot, and other military supplies, and should no more be given back to the rebels than so many cannon or guns. The idea was so pertinent, and the justice of it so plain that the name "contraband" sprang at once into use. But while this happy explanation had more convincing effect on popular thought than a volume of discussion, it did not solve the whole question. By the end of July General Butler had on his hands 900 "contrabands," men, women and children of all ages, and he wrote to inquire what was their real condition. Were they slaves or free? Could they be considered fugitive slaves when their masters had run away and left them? How should they be disposed of? It was a knotty problem, and upon its solution might depend the loyalty or secession of the border slave States of Maryland, West Virginia, Kentucky and Missouri, which, up to that time, had not decided whether to remain in the Union or to cast their fortunes with the South.

In dealing with this perplexing subject. Mr. Lincoln kept in mind one of his favorite stories: the one on the Methodist Presiding Elder who was riding about his circuit during the spring freshets. A young and anxious companion asked how they should ever be able to cross the swollen waters of Fox River, which they were approaching, and the elder quieted him by saying that he made it the rule of his life never to cross Fox River until he came to it. The President, following this rule, did not immediately decide the question, but left it to be treated at the discretion of each commander. Under this theory some commanders admitted black people to their camps, while others refused to receive them. The curt formula of General Orders: "We are neither negro stealers nor negro catchers," was easily read to justify either course. Congress greatly advanced the problem, shortly after the battle of Bull Run, by passing a law which took away a master's right to his slave, when, with his consent, such slave was employed in service or labor hostile to the United States.

On the general question of slavery, the President's mind was fully made up. He felt that he had no right to interfere with slavery where slavery was lawful, just because he himself did not happen to like it; for he had sworn to do all in his power to "preserve, protect and defend" the government and its laws, and slavery was lawful in the southern States. When freeing the slaves should become necessary in order to preserve the Government, then it would be his duty to free them; until that time came, it was equally his duty to let them alone.

Twice during the early part of the war military commanders issued orders freeing slaves in the districts over which they had control, and twice he refused to allow these orders to stand. "No commanding general should do such a thing upon his responsibility, without consulting him," he said; and he added that whether he, as Commander-in-Chief, had the power to free slaves, and whether at any time the use of such power should become necessary, were questions which he reserved to himself. He did not feel justified in leaving such decisions to commanders in the field. He even refused at that time to allow Secretary Cameron to make a public announcement that the government might find it necessary to arm slaves and employ them as soldiers. He would not cross Fox River until he came to it. He would not take any measure until he felt it to be absolutely necessary.

Only a few months later he issued his first proclamation of emancipation; but he did not do so until convinced that he must do this in order to put down the rebellion. Long ago he had considered and in his own mind adopted a plan of dealing with the slavery question--the simple, easy plan which, while a member of Congress, he had proposed for the District of Columbia--that on condition of the slave-owners voluntarily giving up their slaves, they should be paid a fair price for them by the Federal government. Delaware was a slave State, and seemed an excellent place in which to try this experiment of "compensated emancipation," as it was called; for there were, all told, only 1798 slaves left in the State. Without any public announcement of his purpose he offered to the citizens of Delaware, through their representative in Congress, four hundred dollars for each of these slaves, the payment to be made, not all at once, but yearly, during a period of thirty-one years. He believed that if Delaware could be induced to accept this offer, Maryland might follow her example, and that afterward other States would allow themselves to be led along the same easy way. The Delaware House of Representatives voted in favor of the proposition, but five of the nine members of the Delaware senate scornfully repelled the "abolition bribe," as they chose to call it, and the project withered in the bud.

Mr. Lincoln did not stop at this failure, but, on March 6, 1862, sent a special message to the Senate and House of Representatives recommending that Congress adopt a joint resolution favoring and practically offering gradual compensated emancipation to any State that saw fit to accept it; pointing out at the same time that the Federal government claimed no right to interfere with slavery within the States, and that if the offer were accepted it must be done as a matter of free choice.

The Republican journals of the North devoted considerable space to discussing the President's plan, which, in the main, was favorably received; but it was thought that it must fail on the score of expense. The President answered this objection in a private letter to a Senator, proving that less than one-half day's cost of war would pay for all the slaves in Delaware at four hundred dollars each, and less than eighty-seven days' cost of war would pay for all in Delaware, Maryland, the District of Columbia, Kentucky and Missouri. "Do you doubt," he asked, that taking such a step "on the part of those States and this District would shorten the war more than eighty-seven days, and thus be an actual saving of expense?"

Both houses of Congress favored the resolution, and also passed a bill immediately freeing the slaves in the District of Columbia on the payment to their loyal owners of three hundred dollars for each slave. This last bill was signed by the President and became a law on April 16, 1862. So, although he had been unable to bring it about when a member of Congress thirteen years before, it was he, after all, who finally swept away that scandal of the "negro livery-stable" in the shadow of the dome of the Capitol.

Congress as well as the President was thus pledged to compensated emancipation, and if any of the border slave States had shown a willingness to accept the generosity of the government, their people might have been spared the loss that overtook all slave-owners on the first of January, 1863. The President twice called the representatives and senators of these States to the White House, and urged his plan most eloquently, but nothing came of it. Meantime, the military situation continued most discouraging. The advance of the Army of the Potomac upon Richmond became a retreat; the commanders in the West could not get control of the Mississippi River; and worst of all, in spite of their cheering assurance that "We are coming, Father Abraham, three hundred thousand strong," the people of the country were saddened and filled with the most gloomy forebodings because of the President's call for so many new troops.

"It had got to be midsummer, 1862," Mr. Lincoln said, in telling an artist friend the history of his most famous official act. "Things had gone on from bad to worse, until I felt that we had reached the end of our rope on the plan of operations we had been pursuing; that we had about played our last card, and must change our tactics or lose the game. I now determined upon the adoption of the emancipation policy, and without consultation with, or the knowledge of the cabinet, I prepared the original draft of the proclamation, and after much anxious thought, called a cabinet meeting upon the subject. . . . I said to the cabinet that I had resolved upon this step, and had not called them together to ask their advice, but to lay the subject-matter of a proclamation before them, suggestions as to which would be in order after they had heard it read."

It was on July 22 that the President read to his cabinet the draft of this first emancipation proclamation, which, after announcing that at the next meeting of Congress he would again offer compensated emancipation to such States as chose to accept it, went on to order as Commander-in-Chief of the Army and Navy of the United States, that the slaves in all States which should be in rebellion against the government on January 1, 1863, should "then, thenceforward and forever be free."

Mr. Lincoln had given a hint of this intended step to Mr. Seward and Mr. Welles, but to all the other members of the cabinet it came as a complete surprise. One thought it would cost the Republicans the fall elections. Another preferred that emancipation should be proclaimed by military commanders in their several military districts. Secretary Seward, while approving the measure, suggested that it would better be postponed until it could be given to the country after a victory, instead of issuing it, as would be the case then, upon the greatest disasters of the war. "The wisdom of the view of the Secretary of State struck me with very great force," Mr. Lincoln's recital continues. "It was an aspect of the case that, in all my thought upon the subject, I had entirely overlooked. The result was that I put the draft of the proclamation aside, as you do your sketch for a picture, waiting for a victory."

The secrets of the administration were well kept, and no hint came to the public that the President had proposed such a measure to his cabinet. As there was at the moment little in the way of war news to attract attention, newspapers and private individuals turned a sharp fire of criticism upon Mr. Lincoln. For this they seized upon the ever-useful text of the slavery question.

Some of them protested indignantly that the President was going too fast; others clamored as loudly that he had been altogether too slow. His decision, as we know, was unalterably taken, although he was not yet ready to announce it. Therefore, while waiting for a victory he had to perform the difficult task of restraining the impatience of both sides. This he did in very positive language. To a man in Louisiana, who complained that Union feeling was being crushed out by the army in that State, he wrote:

"I am a patient man, always willing to forgive on the Christian terms of repentance, and also to give ample time for repentance. Still, I must save this government if possible. What I cannot do, of course I will not do; but it may as well be understood, once for all, that I shall not surrender this game leaving any available card unplayed." Two days later he answered another Louisiana critic. "What would you do in my position? Would you drop the war where it is? Or would you prosecute it in future with elder-stalk squirts charged with rosewater? Would you deal lighter blows rather than heavier ones? Would you give up the contest leaving any available means unapplied? I am in no boastful mood. I shall not do more than I can, and I shall do all I can, to save the government, which is my sworn duty, as well as my personal inclination. I shall do nothing in malice. What I deal with is too vast for malicious dealing."

The President could afford to overlook the abuse of hostile newspapers, but he also had to meet the criticisms of over-zealous Republicans. The prominent Republican editor, Horace Greeley, printed in his paper, the "New York Tribune," a long "Open Letter," ostentatiously addressed to Mr. Lincoln, full of unjust accusations, his general charge being that the President and many army officers were neglecting their duty through a kindly feeling for slavery. The open letter which Mr. Lincoln wrote in reply is remarkable not alone for the skill with which he answered this attack, but also for its great dignity.

"As to the policy I 'seem to be pursuing,' as you say, I have not meant to leave anyone in doubt. . . . My paramount object in this struggle is to save the Union, and is not either to save or to destroy slavery. If I could save the Union without freeing any slave, I would do it; and if I could save it by freeing all the slaves I would do it; and if I could save it by freeing some and leaving others alone I would also do that. What I do about slavery and the colored race, I do because I believe it helps to save the Union, and what I forbear I forbear because I do not believe it would help to save the Union. I shall do less whenever I shall believe what I am doing hurts the cause, and I shall do more whenever I shall believe doing more will help the cause. I shall try to correct errors when shown to be errors, and I shall adopt new views so fast as they shall appear to be true views. I have here stated my purpose according to my view of official duty, and I intend no modification of my oft-expressed personal wish that all men everywhere could be free."

He was waiting for victory, but victory was slow to come. Instead the Union army suffered another defeat at the second battle of Bull Run on August 30, 1862. After this the pressure upon him to take some action upon slavery became stronger than ever. On September 13 he was visited by a company of ministers from the churches of Chicago, who came expressly to urge him to free the slaves at once. In the actual condition of things he could of course neither safely satisfy them nor deny them, and his reply, while perfectly courteous, had in it a tone of rebuke that showed the state of irritation and high sensitiveness under which he was living:

"I am approached with the most opposite opinions and advice, and that by religious men, who are equally certain that they represent the Divine will. . . . I hope it will not be irreverent for me to say that if it is probable that God would reveal his will to others on a point so connected with my duty, it might be supposed he would reveal it directly to me. . . . What good would a proclamation of emancipation from me do, especially as we are now situated? I do not want to issue a document that the whole world will see must necessarily be inoperative, like the Pope's bull against the comet." "Do not misunderstand me. . . . I have not decided against a proclamation of liberty to the slaves; but hold the matter under advisement. And I can assure you that the subject is on my mind by day and night more than any other. Whatever shall appear to be God's will, I will do."

Four days after this interview the battle of Antietam was fought, and when, after a few days of uncertainty it was found that it could be reasonably claimed as a Union victory, the President resolved to carry out his long-matured purpose. Secretary Chase in his diary recorded very fully what occurred on that ever-memorable September 22, 1862. After some playful talk upon other matters, Mr. Lincoln, taking a graver tone, said:

"Gentlemen: I have, as you are aware, thought a great deal about the relation of this war to slavery, and you all remember that several weeks ago I read to you an order I had prepared on this subject, which, on account of objections made by some of you, was not issued. Ever since then my mind has been much occupied with this subject, and I have thought, all along, that the time for acting on it might probably come. I think the time has come now. I wish it was a better time. I wish that we were in a better condition. The action of the army against the rebels has not been quite what I should have best liked. But they have been driven out of Maryland, and Pennsylvania is no longer in danger of invasion. When the rebel army was at Frederick I determined, as soon as it should be driven out of Maryland, to issue a proclamation of emancipation, such as I thought most likely to be useful. I said nothing to anyone, but I made the promise to myself, and--[hesitating a little]--to my Maker. The rebel army is now driven out, and I am going to fulfil that promise. I have got you together to hear what I have written down. I do not wish your advice about the main matter, for that I have determined for myself. This I say, without intending anything but respect for any one of you. But I already know the views of each on this question. . . . I have considered them as thoroughly and carefully as I can. What I have written is that which my reflections have determined me to say. If there is anything in the expressions I use, or in any minor matter which any one of you thinks had best be changed, I shall be glad to receive the suggestions. One other observation I will make. I know very well that many others might, in this matter as in others, do better than I can; and if I was satisfied that the public confidence was more fully possessed by any one of them than by me, and knew of any constitutional way in which he could be put in my place, he should have it. I would gladly yield it to him. But, though I believe that I have not so much of the confidence of the people as I had some time since, I do not know that, all things considered, any other person has more; and however this may be, there is no way in which I can have any other man put where I am. I am here; I must do the best I can, and bear the responsibility of taking the course which I feel I ought to take."

It was in this humble spirit, and with this firm sense of duty that the great proclamation was given to the world. One hundred days later he completed the act by issuing the final proclamation of emancipation.

It has been a long established custom in Washington for the officials of the government to go on the first day of January to the Executive Mansion to pay their respects to the President and his wife. The judges of the courts go at one hour, the foreign diplomats at another, members of Congress and senators and officers of the Army and Navy at still another. One by one these various official bodies pass in rapid succession before the head of the nation, wishing him success and prosperity in the New Year. The occasion is made gay with music and flowers and bright uniforms, and has a social as well as an official character. Even in war times such customs were kept up, and in spite of his load of care, the President was expected to find time and heart for the greetings and questions and hand-shakings of this and other state ceremonies. Ordinarily it was not hard for him. He liked to meet people, and such occasions were a positive relief from the mental strain of his official work. It is to be questioned, however, whether, on this day, his mind did not leave the passing stream of people before him, to dwell on the proclamation he was so soon to sign.

At about three o'clock in the afternoon, after full three hours of such greetings and handshakings, when his own hand was so weary it could scarcely hold a pen, the President and perhaps a dozen friends, went up to the Executive Office, and there, without any pre-arranged ceremony, he signed his name to the greatest state paper of the century, which banished the curse of slavery from our land, and set almost four million people free.

X. THE MAN WHO WAS PRESIDENT

The way Mr. Lincoln signed this most important state paper was thoroughly in keeping with his nature. He hated all shams and show and pretense, and being absolutely without affectation of any kind, it would never have occurred to him to pose for effect while signing the Emancipation Proclamation or any other paper. He never thought of himself as a President to be set up before a multitude and admired, but always as a President charged with duties which he owed to every citizen. In fulfilling these he did not stand upon ceremony, but took the most direct way to the end he had in view.

It is not often that a President pleads a cause before Congress. Mr. Lincoln did not find it beneath his dignity at one time to go in person to the Capitol, and calling a number of the leading senators and representatives around him, explain to them, with the aid of a map, his reasons for believing that the final stand of the Confederates would be made in that part of the South where the seven States of Virginia, North Carolina, South Carolina, Georgia, Tennessee, Kentucky and West Virginia come together; and strive in this way to interest them in the sad plight of the loyal people of Tennessee who were being persecuted by the Confederate government, but whose mountainous region might, with a little help, be made a citadel of Union strength in the very heart of this stronghold of rebellion.

In his private life he was entirely simple and unaffected. Yet he had a deep sense of what was due his office, and took part with becoming dignity in all official or public ceremonies. He received the diplomats sent to Washington from the courts of Europe with a formal and quiet reserve which made them realize at once that although this son of the people had been born in a log cabin, he was ruler of a great nation, and more than that, was a prince by right of his own fine instincts and good breeding.

He was ever gentle and courteous, but with a few quiet words he could silence a bore who had come meaning to talk to him for hours. For his friends he had always a ready smile and a quaintly turned phrase. His sense of humor was his salvation. Without it he must have died of the strain and anxiety of the

Civil War. There was something almost pathetic in the way he would snatch a moment from his pressing duties and gravest cares to listen to a good story or indulge in a hearty laugh. Some people could not understand this. To one member of his cabinet, at least, it seemed strange and unfitting that he should read aloud to them a chapter from a humorous book by Artemus Ward before taking up the weighty matter of the Emancipation Proclamation. From their point of view it showed lack of feeling and frivolity of character, when, in truth, it was the very depth of his feeling, and the intensity of his distress at the suffering of the war, that led him to seek relief in laughter, to gather from the comedy of life strength to go on and meet its sternest tragedy.

He was a social man. He could not fully enjoy even a jest alone. He wanted somebody to share the pleasure with him. Often when care kept him awake late at night he would wander through the halls of the Executive Mansion, and coming to the room where his secretaries were still at work, would stop to read to them some poem, or a passage from Shakspere, or a bit from one of the humorous books in which he found relief. No one knew better than he what could be cured, and what must be patiently endured. To every difficulty that he could remove he gave cheerful and uncomplaining thought and labor. The burdens he could not shake off he bore with silent courage, lightening them whenever possible with the laughter that he once described as the "universal joyous evergreen of life."

It would be a mistake to suppose that he cared only for humorous reading. Occasionally he read a scientific book with great interest, but his duties left him little time for such indulgences. Few men knew the Bible more thoroughly than he did, and his speeches are full of scriptural quotations. The poem beginning "Oh, why should the spirit of mortal be proud?" was one of his favorites, and Dr. Holmes's "Last Leaf" was another. Shakespere was his constant delight. A copy of Shakespere's works was even to be found in the busy Executive Office, from which most books were banished. The President not only liked to read the great poet's plays, but to see them acted; and when the gifted actor Hackett came to Washington, he was invited to the White House, where the two discussed the character of Falstaff, and the proper reading of many scenes and passages.

While he was President, Mr. Lincoln did not attempt to read the newspapers. His days were long, beginning early and ending late, but they were not long enough for that. One of his secretaries brought him a daily memorandum of the important news they contained. His mail was so enormous that he personally read only about one in every hundred of the letters sent him.

His time was principally taken up with interviews with people on matters of importance, with cabinet meetings, conferences with his generals, and other affairs requiring his close and immediate attention. If he had leisure he would take a drive in the late afternoon, or perhaps steal away into the grounds south of the Executive Mansion to test some new kind of gun, if its inventor had been fortunate enough to bring it to his notice. He was very quick to understand mechanical contrivances, and would often suggest improvements that had not occurred to the inventor himself.

For many years it has been the fashion to call Mr. Lincoln homely. He was very tall, and very thin. His eyes were deep-sunken, his skin of a sallow pallor, his hair coarse, black, and unruly. Yet he was neither ungraceful, nor awkward, nor ugly. His large features fitted his large frame, and his large hands and feet were but right on a body that measured six feet four inches. His was a sad and thoughtful face, and from boyhood he had carried a load of care. It was small wonder that when alone, or absorbed in thought, the face should take on deep lines, the eyes appear as if seeing something beyond the vision of other men, and the shoulders stoop, as though they too were bearing a weight. But in a moment all would be changed. The deep eyes could flash, or twinkle merrily with humor, or look out from under overhanging brows as they did upon the Five Points children in kindliest gentleness. In public speaking, his tall body rose to its full height, his head was thrown back, his face seemed transfigured with the fire and earnestuess of his thought, and his voice took on a high clear tenor tone that carried his words and ideas far out over the listening crowds. At such moments, when answering Douglas in the heat of their joint-debate, or later, during the years of war, when he pronounced with noble gravity the words of his famous addresses, not one in the throngs that heard him could say with truth that he was other than a handsome man.

It has been the fashion, too, to say that he was slovenly, and careless in his dress. This also is a mistake. His clothes could not fit smoothly on his gaunt and bony frame. He was no tailor's figure of a man; but from the first he clothed himself as well as his means allowed, and in the fashion of the time and place. In reading the grotesque stories of his boyhood, of the tall stripling whose trousers left exposed a length of shin, it must be remembered not only how poor he was, but that he lived on the frontier, where other boys, less poor, were scarcely better clad. In Vandalia, the blue jeans he wore was the dress of his companions as well, and later, from Springfield days on, clear through his presidency, his costume was the usual suit of black broadcloth, carefully made, and scrupulously neat. He cared nothing for style. It did not matter to him whether the man with whom he talked wore a coat of the latest cut, or owned no coat at all. It was the man inside the coat that interested him.

In the same way he cared little for the pleasures of the table. He ate most sparingly. He was thankful that food was good and wholesome and enough for daily needs, but he could no more enter into the mood of the epicure for whose palate it is a matter of importance whether he eats roast goose or golden pheasant, than he could have counted the grains of sand under the sea.

In the summers, while he was President, he spent the nights at a cottage at the Soldiers' Home, a short distance north of Washington, riding or driving out through the gathering dusk, and returning to the White House after a frugal breakfast in the early morning. Ten o'clock was the hour at which he was supposed to begin receiving visitors, but it was often necessary to see them unpleasantly early. Occasionally they forced their way to his bedroom before he had quite finished dressing. Throngs of people daily filled his office, the ante-rooms, and even the corridors of the public part of the Executive Mansion. He saw them all, those he had summoned on important business, men of high official position who came to demand as their right offices and favors that he had no right to give; others who wished to offer tiresome if well-meant advice;

and the hundreds, both men and women, who pressed forward to ask all sorts of help. His friends besought him to save himself the weariness of seeing the people at these public receptions, but he refused. "They do not want much, and they get very little," he answered. "Each one considers his business of great importance, and I must gratify them. I know how I would feel if I were in their place." And at noon on all days except Tuesday and Friday, when the time was occupied by meetings of the cabinet, the doors were thrown open, and all who wished might enter. That remark of his, "I know how I would feel if I were in their place," explained it all. His early experience of life had drilled him well for these ordeals. He had read deeply in the book of human nature, and could see the hidden signs of falsehood and deceit and trickery from which the faces of some of his visitors were not free; but he knew, too, the hard, practical side of life, the hunger, cold, storms, sickness and misfortune that the average man must meet in his struggle with the world. More than all, he knew and sympathized with that hope deferred which makes the heart sick.

Not a few men and women came, sad-faced and broken-hearted, to plead for soldier sons or husbands in prison, or under sentence of death by court-martial. An inmate of the White House has recorded the eagerness with which the President caught at any fact that would justify him in saving the life of a condemned soldier. He was only merciless when meanness or cruelty were clearly proved. Cases of cowardice he disliked especially to punish with death. "It would frighten the poor devils too terribly to shoot them," he said. On the papers in the case of one soldier who had deserted and then enlisted again, he wrote: "Let him fight, instead of shooting him."

He used to call these cases of desertion his "leg cases," and sometimes when considering them, would tell the story of the Irish soldier, upbraided by his captain, who replied: "Captain, I have a heart in me breast as brave as Julius Caesar, but when I go into battle, Sor, these cowardly legs of mine will run away with me."

As the war went on, Mr. Lincoln objected more and more to approving sentences of death by court-martial, and either pardoned them outright, or delayed the execution "until further orders," which orders were never given by the great-hearted, merciful man. Secretary Stanton and certain generals complained bitterly that if the President went on pardoning soldiers he would ruin the discipline of the army; but Secretary Stanton had a warm heart, and it is doubtful if he ever willingly enforced the justice that he criticized the President for tempering with so much mercy.

Yet Mr. Lincoln could be sternly just when necessary. A law declaring the slave trade to be piracy had stood on the statute books of the United States for half a century. Lincoln's administration was the first to convict a man under it, and Lincoln himself decreed that the well-deserved sentence be carried out.

Mr. Lincoln sympathized keenly with the hardships and trials of the soldier boys, and found time, amid all his labors and cares, to visit the hospitals in and around Washington where they lay ill. His afternoon drive was usually to some camp in the neighborhood of the city; and when he visited one at a greater distance, the cheers that greeted him as he rode along the line with the commanding general showed what a warm place he held in their hearts.

He did not forget the unfortunate on these visits. A story is told of his interview with William Scott, a boy from a Vermont farm, who, after marching forty-eight hours without sleep, volunteered to stand guard for a sick comrade. Weariness overcame him, and he was found asleep at his post, within gunshot of the enemy. He was tried, and sentenced to be shot. Mr. Lincoln heard of the case, and went himself to the tent where young Scott was kept under guard. He talked to him kindly, asking about his home, his schoolmates, and particularly about his mother. The lad took her picture from his pocket, and showed it to him without speaking. Mr. Lincoln was much affected. As he rose to leave he laid his hand on the prisoner s shoulder. "My boy," he said, "you are not going to be shot to-morrow. I believe you when you tell me that you could not keep awake. I am going to trust you, and send you back to your regiment. Now, I want to know what you intend to pay for all this?" The lad, overcome with gratitude, could hardly say a word, but crowding down his emotions, managed to answer that he did not know. He and his people were poor, they would do what they could. There was his pay, and a little in the savings bank. They could borrow something by a mortgage on the farm. Perhaps his comrades would help. If Mr. Lincoln would wait until pay day possibly they might get together five or six hundred dollars. Would that be enough? The kindly President shook his head. "My bill is a great deal more than that," he said. "It is a very large one. Your friends cannot pay it, nor your family, nor your farm. There is only one man in the world who can pay it, and his name is William Scott. If from this day he does his duty so that when he comes to die he can truly say "I have kept the promise I gave the President. I have done my duty as a soldier,' then the debt will be paid." Young Scott went back to his regiment, and the debt was fully paid a few months later, for he fell in battle.

Mr. Lincoln's own son became a soldier after leaving college. The letter his father wrote to General Grant in his behalf shows how careful he was that neither his official position nor his desire to give his boy the experience he wanted, should work the least injustice to others:

Executive Mansion,

Washington, January 19th, 1865.

Lieutenant-General Grant:

Please read and answer this letter as though I was not President, but only a friend. My son, now in his twenty-second year, having graduated at Harvard, wishes to see something of the war before it ends. I do not wish to put him in the ranks, nor yet to give him a commission, to which those who have already served long are better entitled, and better qualified to hold. Could he, without embarrassment to you, or detriment to the service, go into your military family with some nominal rank, I and not the public furnishing the necessary means? If no, say so without the least hesitation, because I am as anxious and as deeply interested that you shall not be encumbered as you can be yourself.

Yours truly,

A. Lincoln.

His interest did not cease with the life of a young soldier. Among his most beautiful letters are those he wrote to sorrowing parents who had lost their sons in battle; and when his personal friend, young Ellsworth, one of the first and most gallant to fall, was killed at Alexandria, the President directed that his body be brought to the White House, where his funeral was held in the great East Room.

Though a member of no church, Mr. Lincoln was most sincerely religious and devout. Not only was his daily life filled with acts of forbearance and charity; every great state paper that he wrote breathes his faith and reliance on a just and merciful God. He rarely talked, even with intimate friends, about matters of belief, but it is to be doubted whether any among the many people who came to give him advice and sometimes to pray with him, had a better right to be called a Christian. He always received such visitors courteously, with a reverence for their good intention, no matter how strangely it sometimes manifested itself. A little address that he made to some Quakers who came to see him in September, 1862, shows both his courtesy to them personally, and his humble attitude toward God.

"I am glad of this interview, and glad to know that I have your sympathy and prayers. We are indeed going through a great trial, a fiery trial. In the very responsible position in which I happen to be placed, being a humble instrument in the hands of our Heavenly Father as I am, and as we all are, to work out His great purposes, I have desired that all my works and acts may be according to His will, and that it might be so I have sought His aid; but if, after endeavoring to do my best in the light which he affords me, I find my efforts fail, I must believe that for some purpose unknown to me, He wills it otherwise. If I had had my way, this war would never have been commenced. If I had been allowed my way, this war would have been ended before this; but we find it still continues, and we must believe that He permits it for some wise purpose of His own, mysterious and unknown to us; and though with our limited understandings we may not be able to comprehend it, yet we cannot but believe that He who made the world still governs it."

Children held a warm place in the President's affections. He was not only a devoted father; his heart went out to all little folk. He had been kind to babies in his boyish days, when, book in hand, and the desire for study upon him, he would sit with one foot on the rocker of a rude frontier cradle, not too selfishly busy to keep its small occupant lulled and content, while its mother went about her household tasks. After he became President many a sad-eyed woman carrying a child in her arms went to see him, and the baby always had its share in gaining her a speedy hearing, and if possible a favorable answer to her petition.

When children came to him at the White House of their own accord, as they sometimes did, the favors they asked were not refused because of their youth. One day a small boy, watching his chance, slipped into the Executive Office between a governor and a senator, when the door was opened to admit them. They were as much astonished at seeing him there as the President was, and could not explain his presence; but he spoke for himself. He had come, he said, from a little country town, hoping to get a place as page in the House of Representatives. The President began to tell him that he must go to Captain Goodnow, the doorkeeper of the House, for he himself had nothing to do with such appointments. Even this did not discourage the little fellow. Very earnestly he pulled his papers of recommendation out of his pocket, and Mr. Lincoln, unable to resist his wistful face, read them, and sent him away happy with a hurried line written on the back of them, saying: "If Captain Goodnow can give this good little boy a place, he will oblige A. Lincoln."

It was a child who persuaded Mr. Lincoln to wear a beard. Up to the time he was nominated for President he had always been smooth-shaven. A little girl living in Chautauqua County, New York, who greatly admired him, made up her mind that he would look better if he wore whiskers, and with youthful directness wrote and told him so. He answered her by return mail:

Springfield, ILL., Oct. 19, 1860.

Miss Grace Bedelt,

My dear little Miss: Your very agreeable letter of the fifteenth is received. I regret the necessity of saying I have no daughter. I have three sons, one seventeen, one nine, and one seven years of age. They, with their mother, constitute my whole family. As to the whiskers, never having worn any, do you not think people would call it a piece of silly affectation if I were to begin now?

Your very sincere well-wisher,

A. Lincoln.

Evidently on second thoughts he decided to follow her advice. On his way to Washington his train stopped at the town where she lived. He asked if she were in the crowd gathered at the station to meet him. Of course she was, and willing hands forced a way for her through the mass of people. When she reached the car Mr. Lincoln stepped from the train, kissed her, and showed her that he had taken her advice.

The Secretary who wrote about the President's desire to save the lives of condemned soldiers tells us that "during the first year of the administration the house was made lively by the games and pranks of Mr. Lincoln's two younger children, William and Thomas. Robert the eldest was away at Harvard, only coming home for short vacations. The two little boys, aged eight and ten, with their western independence and enterprise, kept the house in an uproar. They drove their tutor wild with their good-natured disobedience. They organized a minstrel show in the attic; they made acquaintance with the office-seekers and became the hot champions of the distressed. William was, with all his boyish frolic, a child of great promise, capable of close application and study. He had a fancy for drawing up railway time-tables, and would conduct an imaginary train from Chicago to New York with perfect precision. He wrote childish verses, which sometimes attained the unmerited honors of print. But this bright, gentle and studious child sickened and died in February, 1862. His father was profoundly moved by his death, though he gave no outward sign of his trouble, but kept about his work, the same as ever. His bereaved heart seemed afterwards to pour out its fulness on his youngest child. 'Tad' was a merry, warm-blooded, kindly little boy, perfectly lawless, and full of odd fancies and inventions, the 'chartered libertine' of the Executive Mansion." He ran constantly in and out of his father's office, interrupting his gravest labors. Mr. Lincoln was never too busy to hear him, or to answer his bright, rapid, imperfect speech, for he was not able to speak plainly until he was nearly grown. "He would perch upon his father's knee, and sometimes even on his shoulder, while the most weighty conferences were going on. Sometimes, escaping from the domestic authorities, he would take refuge in that sanctuary for the whole evening, dropping to sleep at last on the floor, when the President would pick him up, and carry him tenderly to bed."

The letters and even the telegrams Mr. Lincoln sent his wife had always a message for or about Tad. One of them shows that his pets, like their young master, were allowed great liberty. It was written when the family was living at the Soldiers' Home, and Mrs. Lincoln and Tad had gone away for a visit. "Tell dear Tad," he wrote, "that poor Nanny Goat is lost, and Mrs. Cuthbert and I are in distress about it. The day you left, Nanny was found resting herself and chewing her little cud on the middle of Tad's bed; but now she's gone! The gardener kept complaining that she destroyed the flowers, till it was concluded to bring her down to the White House. This was done, and the second day she had disappeared and has not been heard of since. This is the last we know of poor Nanny."

Tad was evidently consoled by, not one, but a whole family of new goats, for about a year later Mr. Lincoln ended a business telegram to his wife in New York with the words: "Tell Tad the goats and Father are very well." Then, as the weight of care rolled back upon this greathearted, patient man, he added, with humorous weariness, "especially the goats."

Mr. Lincoln was so forgetful of self as to be absolutely without personal fear. He not only paid no attention to the threats which were constantly made against his life, but when, on July 11, 1864, the Confederate General Early appeared suddenly and unexpectedly before the city with a force of 17,000 men, and Washington was for two days actually in danger of assault and capture, his unconcern gave his friends great uneasiness. On the tenth he rode out, as was his custom, to spend the night at the Soldiers' Home, but Secretary Stanton, learning that Early was advancing, sent after him, to compel his return. Twice afterward, intent upon watching the fighting which took place near Fort Stevens, north of the city, he exposed his tall form to the gaze and bullets of the enemy, utterly heedless of his own peril; and it was not until an officer had fallen mortally wounded within a few feet of him, that he could be persuaded to seek a place of greater safety.

XI. THE TURNING POINT OF THE WAR

In the summer of 1863 the Confederate armies reached their greatest strength. It was then that, flushed with military ardor, and made bold by what seemed to the southern leaders an unbroken series of victories on the Virginia battlefields, General Lee again crossed the Potomac River, and led his army into the North. He went as far as Gettysburg in Pennsylvania; but there, on the third of July, 1863, suffered a disastrous defeat, which shattered forever the Confederate dream of taking Philadelphia and dictating peace from Independence Hall. This battle of Gettysburg should have ended the war, for General Lee, on retreating southward, found the Potomac River so swollen by heavy rains that he was obliged to wait several days for the floods to go down. In that time it would have been quite possible for General Meade, the Union commander, to follow him and utterly destroy his army. He proved too slow, however, and Lee and his beaten Confederate soldiers escaped. President Lincoln was inexpressibly grieved at this, and in the first bitterness of his disappointment sat down and wrote General Meade a letter. Lee "was within your easy grasp," he told him, "and to have closed upon him would, in connection with our other late successes, have ended the war. As it is, the war will be prolonged indefinitely. . . . Your golden opportunity is gone and I am distressed immeasurably because of it." But Meade never received this letter. Deeply as the President felt Meade's fault, his spirit of forgiveness was so quick, and his thankfulness for the measure of success that had been gained, so great, that he put it in his desk, and it was never signed or sent.

The battle of Gettysburg was indeed a notable victory, and coupled with the fall of Vicksburg, which surrendered to General Grant on that same third of July, proved the real turning-point of the war. It seems singularly appropriate, then, that Gettysburg should have been the place where President Lincoln made his most beautiful and famous address. After the battle the dead and wounded of both the Union and Confederate armies had received tender attention there. Later it was decided to set aside a portion of the battlefield for a great national military cemetery in which the dead found orderly burial. It was dedicated to its sacred use on November 19, 1863. At the end of the stately ceremonies President Lincoln rose and said:

"Fourscore and seven years ago our fathers brought forth on this continent a new nation, conceived in liberty, and dedicated to the proposition that all men are created equal.

"Now we are engaged in a great civil war, testing whether that nation, or any nation, so conceived and so dedicated, can long endure. We are met on a great battlefield of that war. We have come to dedicate a portion of that field as a final resting place for those who here gave their lives that that nation might live. It is altogether fitting and proper that we should do this.

"But in a larger sense, we cannot dedicate--we cannot consecrate- -we cannot hallow--this ground. The brave men, living and dead, who struggled here have consecrated it far above our poor power to add or detract. The world will little note nor long remember what we say here, but it can never forget what they did here. It is for us the living, rather, to be dedicated here to the unfinished work which they who fought here have thus far so nobly advanced. It is rather for us to be here dedicated to the great task remaining before us--that from these honored dead we take increased devotion to that cause for which they gave the last full measure of devotion; that we here highly resolve that these dead shall not have died in vain; that this nation, under God, shall have a new birth of freedom, and that government of the people, by the people, for the people, shall not perish from the earth."

With these words, so brief, so simple, so full of reverent feeling, he set aside the place of strife to be the resting place of heroes, and then went back to his own great task--for which he, too, was to give "the last full measure of devotion."

Up to within a very short time little had been heard about Ulysses S. Grant, the man destined to become the most successful general of the war. Like General McClellan, he was a graduate of West Point; and also like McClellan, he had resigned from the army after serving gallantly in the Mexican war. There the resemblance ceased, for he had not an atom of McClellan's vanity, and his persistent will to do the best he could with the means the government could give him was far removed from the younger general's faultfinding and complaint. He was about four years older than McClellan, having been born on April 27, 1822. On offering his services to the War Department in 1861 he had modestly written: "I feel myself competent to command a regiment if the President in his judgment should see fit to intrust one to me." For some reason this letter remained unanswered, although the Department, then and later, had need of trained and experienced officers. Afterward the Governor of Illinois made him a colonel of one of the three years' volunteer regiments; and from that time on he rose in rank, not as McClellan had done, by leaps and bounds, but slowly, earning every promotion. All of his service had been in the West, and he first came into general notice by his persistent and repeated efforts to capture Vicksburg, on whose fall the opening of the Mississippi River depended. Five different plans he tried before he finally succeeded, the last one appearing utterly foolhardy, and seeming to go against every known rule of military science. In spite of this it was successful, the Union army and navy thereby gaining control of the Mississippi River and cutting off forever from the Confederacy a great extent of rich country, from which, up to that time, it had been drawing men and supplies.

The North was greatly cheered by these victories, and all eyes were turned upon the successful commander. No one was more thankful than Mr. Lincoln. He gave Grant quick promotion, and crowned the official act with a most generous letter. "I do not remember that you and I ever met personally," he wrote. "I write this now as a grateful acknowledgement for the almost inestimable service you have done the country. I wish to say a word further." Then, summing up the plans that the General had tried, especially the last one, he added: "I feared it was a mistake. I now wish to make the personal acknowledgement that you were right and I was wrong."

Other important battles won by Grant that same fall added to his growing fame, and by the beginning of 1864 he was singled out as the greatest Union commander. As a suitable reward for his victories it was determined to make him Lieutenant-General. This army rank had, before the Civil War, been bestowed on only two American soldiers--on General Washington, and on Scott, for his conquest of Mexico. In 1864 Congress passed and the President signed an act to revive the grade, and Grant was called to Washington to receive his commission. He and Mr. Lincoln met for the first time at a large public reception held at the Executive Mansion on the evening of March 8. A movement and rumor in the crowd heralded his approach, and when at last the short, stocky, determined soldier and the tall, care-worn, deep-eyed President stood face to face the crowd, moved by a sudden impulse of delicacy, drew back, and left them almost alone to exchange a few words. Later, when Grant appeared in the great East Room, the enthusiasm called forth by his presence could no longer be restrained, and cheer after cheer went up, while his admirers pressed about him so closely that, hot and blushing with embarrassment, he was forced at last to mount a sofa, and from there shake hands with the eager people who thronged up to him from all sides.

The next day at one o'clock the President, in the presence of the cabinet and a few other officials, made a little speech, and gave him his commission. Grant replied with a few words, as modest as they were brief, and in conversation afterward asked what special duty was required of him. The President answered that the people wanted him to take Richmond, and asked if he could do it. Grant said that he could if he had the soldiers, and the President promised that these would be furnished him. Grant did not stay in Washington to enjoy the new honors of his high rank, but at once set about preparations for his task. It proved a hard one. More than a year passed before it was ended, and all the losses in battle of the three years that had gone before seemed small in comparison with the terrible numbers of killed and wounded that fell during these last months of the war. At first Grant had a fear that the President might wish to control his plans, but this was soon quieted; and his last lingering doubt on the subject vanished when, as he was about to start on his final campaign, Mr. Lincoln sent him a letter stating his satisfaction with all he had done, and assuring him that in the coming campaign he neither knew, for desired to know, the details of his plans. In his reply Grant confessed the groundlessness of his fears, and added, "Should my success be less than I desire and expect, the least I can say is, the fault is not with you."

He made no complicated plan for the problem before him, but proposed to solve it by plain, hard, persistent fighting. "Lee's army will be your objective point," he instructed General Meade. "Where Lee goes there you will go also." Nearly three years earlier the opposing armies had fought their first battle of Bull Run only a short distance north of where they now confronted each other. Campaign and battle between them had swayed to the north and the south, but neither could claim any great gain of ground or of advantage. The final struggle was before them. Grant had two to one in numbers; Lee the advantage in position, for he knew by heart every road, hill and forest in Virginia, had for his friendly scout every white inhabitant, and could retire into prepared fortifications. Perhaps the greatest element of his strength lay in the conscious pride of his army that for three years it had steadily barred the way to Richmond. To offset this there now menaced it what had always been absent before--the grim, unflinching will of the new Union commander, who had rightly won for himself the name of "Unconditional Surrender" Grant.

On the night of May 4, 1864, his army entered upon the campaign which, after many months, was to end the war. It divided itself into two parts. For the first six weeks there was almost constant swift marching and hard fighting, a nearly equally matched contest of strategy and battle between the two armies, the difference being that Grant was always advancing, and Lee always retiring. Grant had hoped to defeat Lee outside of his fortifications, and early in the campaign had expressed his resolution "to fight it out on this line if it takes all summer"; but the losses were so appalling, 60,000 of his best troops melting away in killed and wounded during the six weeks, that this was seen to be impossible. Lee's army was therefore driven into its fortifications around the Confederate capital and then came the siege of Richmond, lasting more than nine months, but pushed forward all that time with relentless energy, in spite of Grant's heavy losses.

In the West, meanwhile, General William T. Sherman, Grant's closest friend and brother officer, pursued a task of almost equal importance, taking Atlanta, Georgia, which the Confederates had turned into a city of foundries and workshops for the manufacture and repair of guns; then, starting from Atlanta, marching with his best troops three hundred miles to the sea, laying the country waste as they went; after which, turning northward, he led them through South and North Carolina to bring his army in touch with Grant.

Against this background of fighting the life of the country went on. The end of the war was approaching, surely, but so slowly that the people, hoping for it, and watching day by day, could scarcely see it. They schooled themselves to a dogged endurance, but there was no more enthusiasm. Many lost courage. Volunteering almost ceased, and the government was obliged to begin drafting men to make up the numbers of soldiers needed by Grant in his campaign against Richmond.

The President had many things to dishearten him at this time, many troublesome questions to settle. For instance, there were new loyal State governments to provide in those parts of the South which had again come under control of the Union armies--no easy matter, where every man, woman and child harbored angry feelings against the North, and no matter how just and forbearing he might be, his plans were sure to be thwarted and bitterly opposed at every step.

There were serious questions, too, to be decided about negro soldiers, for the South had raised a mighty outcry against the Emancipation Proclamation, especially against the use of the freed slaves as soldiers, vowing that white officers of negro troops would be shown small mercy, if ever they were taken prisoners. No act of such vengeance occurred, but in 1864 a fort manned by colored soldiers was captured by the Confederates, and almost the entire garrison was put to death. Must the order that the War Department had issued some time earlier, to offset the Confederate threats, now be put in force? The order said that for every negro prisoner killed by the Confederates a Confederate prisoner in the hands of the Union armies would be taken out and shot. It fell upon Mr. Lincoln to decide. The idea seemed unbearable to him, yet, on the other hand, could he afford to let the massacre go unavenged and thus encourage the South in the belief that it could commit such barbarous acts and escape unharmed? Two reasons finally decided him against putting the order in force. One was that General Grant was about to start on his campaign against Richmond, and that it would be most unwise to begin this by the tragic spectacle of a military punishment, however merited. The other was his tender-hearted humanity. He could not, he said, take men out and kill them in cold blood for crimes committed by other men. If he could get hold of the persons who were guilty of killing the colored prisoners in cold blood, the case would be different; but he could not kill the innocent for the guilty. Fortunately the offense was not repeated, and no one had cause to criticize his clemency.

Numbers of good and influential men, dismayed at the amount of blood and treasure that the war had already cost, and disheartened by the calls for still more soldiers that Grant's campaign made necessary, began to clamor for peace--were ready to grant almost anything that the Confederates chose to ask. Rebel agents were in Canada professing to be able to conclude a peace. Mr. Lincoln, wishing to convince these northern "Peace men" of the groundlessness of their claim, and of the injustice of their charges that the government was continuing the war unnecessarily, sent Horace Greeley, the foremost among them, to Canada, to talk with the selfstyled ambassadors of Jefferson Davis. Nothing came of it, of course, except abuse of Mr. Lincoln for sending such a messenger, and a lively quarrel between Greeley and the rebel agents as to who was responsible for the misunderstandings that arose.

The summer and autumn of 1864 were likewise filled with the bitterness and high excitement of a presidential campaign; for, according to law, Mr. Lincoln's successor had to be elected on the "Tuesday after the first Monday" of November in that year. The great mass of Republicans wished Mr. Lincoln to be reelected. The Democrats had long ago fixed upon General McClellan, with his grievances against the President, as their future candidate. It is not unusual for Presidents to discover would-be rivals in their own cabinets. Considering the strong men who formed Mr. Lincoln's cabinet, and the fact that four years earlier more than one of them had active hopes of being chosen in his stead, it is remarkable that there was so little of this.

The one who developed the most serious desire to succeed him was Salmon P. Chase, his Secretary of the Treasury. Devoted with all his powers to the cause of the Union, Mr. Chase was yet strangely at fault in his judgment of men. He regarded himself as the friend of Mr. Lincoln, but nevertheless held so poor an opinion of the President's mind and character, compared with his own, that he could not believe people blind enough to prefer the President to himself. He imagined that he did not want the office, and was anxious only for the public good; yet he listened eagerly to the critics of the President who flattered his hopes, and found time in spite of his great labors to write letters to all parts of the country, which, although protesting that he did not want the honor, showed his entire willingness to accept it. Mr. Lincoln was well aware of this. Indeed, it was impossible not to know about it, though he refused to hear the matter discussed or to read any letters concerning it. He had his own opinion of the taste displayed by Mr. Chase, but chose to take no notice of his actions. "I have determined," he said, "to shut my eyes, so far as possible, to everything of the sort. Mr. Chase makes a good Secretary, and I shall keep him where he is. If he becomes President, all right. I hope we may never have a worse man, and he not only kept him where he was, but went on appointing Chase's friends to office.

There was also some talk of making General Grant the Republican candidate for President, and an attempt was even made to trap Mr. Lincoln into taking part in a meeting where this was to be done. Mr. Lincoln refused to attend, and instead wrote a letter of such hearty and generous approval of Grant and his army that the meeting naturally fell into the hands of Mr. Lincoln's friends. General Grant, never at that time or any other, gave the least encouragement to the efforts which were made to array him against the President Mr. Lincoln, on his part, received all warnings to beware of Grant in the most serene manner, saying tranquilly, "If he takes Richmond, let him have it." It was not so with General Fremont. At a poorly attended meeting held in Cleveland he was actually nominated by a handful of people calling themselves the "Radical Democracy," and taking the matter seriously, accepted, although, three months later, having found no response from the public, he withdrew from the contest.

After all, these various attempts to discredit the name of Abraham Lincoln caused hardly a ripple on the great current of public opinion, and death alone could have prevented his choice by the Republican national convention. He took no measures to help on his own candidacy. With strangers he would not talk about the probability of his reelection; but with friends he made no secret of his readiness to continue the work he was engaged in if such should be the general wish. "A second term would be a great honor and a great labor; which together, perhaps, I would not decline," he wrote to one of them. He discouraged officeholders, either civil or military, who showed any special zeal in his behalf. To General Schurz, who wrote asking permission to take an active part in the campaign for his reelection, he answered: "I perceive no objection to your making a political speech when you are where one is to be made; but quite surely, speaking in the North and fighting in the South at the same time are not possible, nor could I be justified to detail any officer to the political campaign . . . and then return him to the army."

He himself made no long speeches during the summer, and in his short addresses, at Sanitary Fairs, in answer to visiting delegations, and on similar occasions where custom and courtesy obliged him to say a few words, he kept his quiet ease and self-command, speaking heartily and to the point, yet avoiding all the pitfalls that beset the candidate who talks.

When the Republican national convention came together in Baltimore on June 7, 1864, it had very little to do, for its delegates were bound by rigid instructions to vote for Abraham Lincoln.

He was chosen on the first ballot, every State voting for him except Missouri, whose representatives had been instructed to vote for Grant. Missouri at once changed its vote, and the secretary of the convention read the grand total of 506 for Lincoln, his announcement being greeted by a storm of cheers that lasted several minutes.

It was not so easy to choose a Vice-President. Mr. Lincoln had been besieged by many people to make known his wishes in the matter, but had persistently refused. He rightly felt that it would be presumptuous in him to dictate who should be his companion on the ticket, and, in case of his death, his successor in office. This was for the delegates to the convention to decide, for they represented the voters of the country. He had no more right to dictate who should be selected than the Emperor of China would have had. It is probable that Vice-President Hamlin would have been renominated, if it had not been for the general feeling both in and out of the convention that, under all the circumstances, it would be wiser to select some man who had been a Democrat, and had yet upheld the war. The choice fell upon Andrew Johnson of Tennessee, who was not only a Democrat, but had been appointed by Mr. Lincoln military governor of Tennessee in 1862.

The Democrats at first meant to have the national convention of their party meet on the fourth of July; but after Fremont had been nominated at Cleveland and Lincoln at Baltimore, they postponed it to a later date, hoping that something in the chapter of accidents might happen to their advantage. At first it appeared as if this might be the case. The outlook for the Republicans was far from satisfactory. The terrible fighting and great losses of Grant's army in Virginia had profoundly shocked and depressed the country. The campaign of General Sherman, who was then in Georgia, showed as yet no promise of the brilliant results it afterward attained. General Early's sudden raid into Maryland, when he appeared so unexpectedly before Washington and threatened the city, had been the cause of much exasperation; and Mr. Chase, made bitter by his failure to receive the coveted nomination for President, had resigned from the cabinet. This seemed, to certain leading Republicans, to point to a breaking up of the government. The "Peace" men were clamoring loudly for an end of the war; and the Democrats, not having yet formally chosen a candidate, were free to devote all their leisure to attacks upon the administration.

Mr. Lincoln realized fully the tremendous issues at stake. He looked worn and weary. To a friend who urged him to go away for a fortnight's rest, he replied, "I cannot fly from my thoughts. My solicitude for this great country follows me wherever I go. I do not think it is personal vanity or ambition, though I am not free from these infirmities, but I cannot but feel that the weal or woe of this great nation will be decided in November. There is no program offered by any wing of the Democratic party but that must result in the permanent destruction of the Union."

The political situation grew still darker. Toward the end of August the general gloom enveloped even the President himself. Then what he did was most original and characteristic. Feeling that the campaign was going against him, he made up his mind deliberately the course he ought to pursue, and laid down for himself the action demanded by his strong sense of duty. He wrote on August 23 the following memorandum: "This morning, as for some days past, it seems exceedingly probable that this administration will not be reelected. Then it will be my duty to so cooperate with the President-elect as to save the Union between the election and the inauguration, as he will have secured his election on such ground that he cannot possibly save it afterward."

He folded and pasted the sheet of paper in such a way that its contents could not be seen, and as the cabinet came together handed it to each member successively, asking him to write his name across the back of it. In this peculiar fashion he pledged himself and his administration to accept loyally the verdict of the people if it should be against them, and to do their utmost to save the Union in the brief remainder of his term of office. He gave no hint to any member of his cabinet of the nature of the paper thus signed until after his reelection.

The Democratic convention finally came together in Chicago on August 29. It declared the war a failure, and that efforts ought to be made at once to bring it to a close, and nominated General McClellan for President McClellan's only chance of success lay in his war record. His position as a candidate on a platform of dishonorable peace would have been no less desperate than ridiculous. In his letter accepting the nomination, therefore, he calmly ignored the platform, and renewed his assurances of devotion to the Union, the Constitution, and the flag of his country. But the stars in their courses fought against him. Even before the Democratic convention met, the tide of battle had turned. The darkest hour of the war had passed, and dawn was at hand, and amid the thanksgivings of a grateful people, and the joyful salute of great guns, the real presidential campaign began. The country awoke to the true meaning of the Democratic platform; General Sherman's successes in the South excited the enthusiasm of the people; and when at last the Unionists, rousing from their midsummer languor, began to show their faith in the Republican candidate, the hopelessness of all efforts to undermine him became evident.

XII. THE CONQUEROR OF A GREAT REBELLION

The presidential election of 1864 took place on November 8. The diary of one of the President's secretaries contains a curious record of the way the day passed at the Executive Mansion. "The house has been still and almost deserted. Everybody in Washington and not at home voting seems ashamed of it, and stays away from the President. While I was talking with him to-day he said: "It is a little singular that I, who am not a vindictive man, should always have been before the people for election in canvasses marked for their bitterness. Always but once. When I came to Congress it was a quiet time; but always besides that the contests in which I have been prominent have been marked with great rancor."

Early in the evening the President made his way through rain and darkness to the War Department to receive the returns. The telegrams came, thick and fast, all pointing joyously to his reelection. He sent the important ones over to Mrs. Lincoln at the White House, remarking, "She is more anxious that I am." The satisfaction of one member of the little group about him was coupled with the wish that the critics of the administration might feel properly rebuked by this strong expression of the popular will. Mr. Lincoln looked at him in kindly surprise. "You have more of that feeling of personal resentment than I," he said. "Perhaps I have too little of it, but I never thought it paid. A man has not time to spend half his life in quarrels. If any man ceases to attack me, I never remember the past against him." This state of mind might well have been called by a higher name than "lack of personal resentment."

Lincoln and Johnson received a popular majority of 411,281, and 212 out of 233 electoral votes--only those of New Jersey, Delaware and Kentucky, twenty-one in all, being cast for McClellan.

For Mr. Lincoln this was one of the most solemn days of his life. Assured of his personal success, and made devoutly confident by the military victories of the last few weeks that the end of the war was at hand, he felt no sense of triumph over his opponents. The thoughts that filled his mind found expression in the closing sentences of the little speech that he made to some serenaders who greeted him in the early morning hours of November 9, as he left the War Department to return to the White House:

"I am thankful to God for this approval of the people; but while deeply grateful for this mark of their confidence in me, if I know my heart, my gratitude is free from any taint of personal triumph. . . . It is no pleasure to me to triumph over anyone, but I give thanks to the Almighty for this evidence of the people's resolution to stand by free government and the rights of humanity."

Mr. Lincoln's inauguration for his second term as President took place at the time appointed, on March 4, 1865. There is little variation in the simple but impressive pageantry with which the ceremony is celebrated. The principal novelty commented on by the newspapers was the share which the people who had up to that time been slaves, had for the first time in this public and political drama. Associations of negro citizens joined in the procession, and a battalion of negro soldiers formed part of the military escort. The central act of the occasion was President Lincoln's second inaugural address, which enriched the political literature of the nation with another masterpiece. He said:

"Fellow-countrymen: At this second appearing to take the oath of the presidential office, there is less occasion for an extended address than there was at the first. Then a statement, somewhat in detail, of a course to be pursued, seemed fitting and proper. Now, at the expiration of four years, during which public declarations have been constantly called forth on every point and phase of the great contest which still absorbs the attention and engrosses the energies of the nation, little that is new could be presented. The progress of our arms, upon which all else chiefly depends, is as well known to the public as to myself; and it is, I trust, reasonably satisfactory and encouraging to all. With high hope for the future, no prediction in regard to it is ventured.

"On the occasion corresponding to this four years ago, all thoughts were anxiously directed to an impending civil war. All dreaded it--all sought to avert it. While the inaugural address was being delivered from this place, devoted altogether to saving the Union without war, insurgent agents were in the city seeking to destroy it without war--seeking to dissolve the Union and divide effects, by negotiation. Both parties deprecated war; but one of them would make war rather than let the nation survive; and the other would accept war rather than let it perish. And the war came.

"One-eighth of the whole population were colored slaves, not distributed generally over the Union, but localized in the southern part of it. These slaves constituted a peculiar and powerful interest. All knew that this interest was, somehow, the cause of the war. To strengthen, perpetuate and extend this interest was the object for which the insurgents would rend the Union, even by war; while the government claimed no right to do more than to restrict the territorial enlargement of it.

"Neither party expected for the war the magnitude or the duration which it has already attained. Neither anticipated that the cause of the conflict might cease with, or even before, the conflict itself should cease. Each looked for an easier triumph, and a result less fundamental and astounding. Both read the same Bible, and pray to the same God; and each invokes his aid against the other. It may seem strange that any men should dare to ask a just God's assistance in wringing their bread from the sweat of other men's faces; but let us judge not, that we be not judged. The prayers of both could not be answered--that of neither has been answered fully.

"The Almighty has his own purposes. 'Woe unto the world because of offenses! For it must needs be that offenses come; but woe to that man by whom the offense cometh.' If we shall suppose that American slavery is one of those offenses which, in the providence of God, must needs come, but which, having continued through his appointed time, he now wills to remove, and that he gives to both North and South this terrible war, as the woe due to those by whom the offense came, shall we discern therein any departure from those divine attributes which the believers in a living God always ascribe to him? Fondly do we hope--fervently do we pray--that this mighty scourge of war may speedily pass away. Yet; if God wills that it continue until all the wealth piled by the bondman's two hundred and fifty years of unrequited toil shall be sunk, and until every drop of blood drawn with the lash shall be paid by another drawn with the sword, as was said three thousand years ago, so still it must be said, 'The judgments of the Lord are true and righteous altogether.'

"With malice toward none; with charity for all; with firmness in the right, as God gives us to see the right, let us strive on to finish the work we are in; to bind up the nation's wounds; to care for him who shall have borne the battle, and for his widow, and his orphan--to do all which may achieve and cherish a just and lasting peace among ourselves, and with all nations."

The address ended, the Chief Justice arose, and the listeners who, for the second time, heard Abraham Lincoln repeat the solemn words of his oath of office, went from the impressive scene to their several homes in thankfulness and confidence that the destiny of the nation was in safe keeping.

Nothing would have amazed Mr. Lincoln more than to hear himself called a man of letters; and yet it would be hard to find in all literature anything to excel the brevity and beauty of his address at Gettysburg or the lofty grandeur of this Second Inaugural. In Europe his style has been called a model for the study and imitation of princes, while in our own country many of his phrases have already passed into the daily speech of mankind.

His gift of putting things simply and clearly was partly the habit of his own clear mind, and partly the result of the training he gave himself in days of boyish poverty, when paper and ink were luxuries almost beyond his reach, and the words he wished to set down must be the best words, and the clearest and shortest to express the ideas he had in view. This training of thought before expression, of knowing exactly what he wished to say before saying it, stood him in good stead all his life; but only the mind of a great man, with a lofty soul and a poet's vision; one who had suffered deeply and felt keenly; who carried the burden of a nation on his heart, whose sympathies were as broad and whose kindness was as great as his moral purpose was strong and firm, could have written the deep, forceful, convincing words that fell from his pen in the later years of his life. It was the life he lived, the noble aim that upheld him, as well as the genius with which he was born, that made him one of the greatest writers of our time.

At the date of his second inauguration only two members of Mr. Lincoln's original cabinet remained in office; but the changes had all come about gradually and naturally, never as the result of quarrels, and with the single exception of Secretary Chase, not one of them left the cabinet harboring feelings of resentment or bitterness toward his late chief. Even when, in one case, it became necessary for the good of the service, for Mr. Lincoln to ask a cabinet minister to resign, that gentleman not only unquestioningly obeyed, but entered into the presidential campaign immediately afterward, working heartily and effectively for his reelection. As for Secretary Chase, the President was so little disturbed by his attitude that, on the death of Roger B. Taney, the Chief Justice of the United States Supreme Court, he made him his successor, giving him the highest judicial office in the land, and paying him the added compliment of writing out his nomination with his own hand.

The keynote of the President's young life had been persevering industry. That of his mature years was self-control and generous forgiveness. And surely his remark on the night of his second election for President, that he did not think resentment "paid," and that no man had time to spend half his life in quarrels, was well borne out by the fruit of his actions. It was this spirit alone which made possible much that he was able to accomplish. His rule of conduct toward all men is summed up in a letter of reprimand that it became his duty, while he was President, to send to one young officer accused of quarreling with another. It deserves to be written in letters of gold on the walls of every school and college throughout the land:

"The advice of a father to his son, 'beware of entrance to a quarrel, but, being in, bear it that the opposed may beware of thee,' is good, but not the best. Quarrel not at all. No man resolved to make the most of himself can spare time for personal contention. Still less can he afford to take all the consequences, including the vitiating of his temper and the loss of self-control. Yield larger things to which you can show no more than equal right; and yield lesser ones though clearly your own. Better give your path to a dog than be bitten by him in contesting for the right. Even killing the dog would not cure the bite."

It was this willingness of his to give up the "lesser things," and even the things to which he could claim an equal right, which kept peace in his cabinet, made up of men of strong wills and conflicting natures. Their devotion to the

Union, great as it was, would not have sufficed in such a strangely assorted official family; but his unfailing kindness and good sense led him to overlook many things that another man might have regarded as deliberate insults; while his great tact and knowledge of human nature enabled him to bring out the best in people about him, and at times to turn their very weaknesses into sources of strength. It made it possible for him to keep the regard of every one of them. Before he had been in office a month it had transformed Secretary Seward from his rival into his lasting friend. It made a warm friend out of the blunt, positive, hot-tempered Edwin M. Stanton, who became Secretary of War in place of Mr. Cameron. He was a man of strong will and great endurance, and gave his Department a record for hard and effective work that it would be difficult to equal. Many stories are told of the disrespect he showed the President, and the cross-purposes at which they labored. The truth is, that they understood each other perfectly on all important matters, and worked together through three busy trying years with ever-increasing affection and regard. The President's kindly humor forgave his Secretary many blunt speeches. "Stanton says I am a fool?" he is reported to have asked a busy-body who came fleet-footed to tell him of the Secretary's hasty comment on an order of little moment. "Stanton says I am a fool? Well"--with a whimsical glance at his informant--"then I suppose I must be. Stanton is nearly always right." Knowing that Stanton was "nearly always right" it made little difference to his chief what he might say in the heat of momentary annoyance.

Yet in spite of his forbearance he never gave up the "larger things" that he felt were of real importance; and when he learned at one time that an effort was being made to force a member of the cabinet to resign, he called them together, and read them the following impressive little lecture:

"I must myself be the judge how long to retain in, and when to remove any of you from his position. It would greatly pain me to discover any of you endeavoring to procure another's removal, or in any way to prejudice him before the public. Such endeavor would be a wrong to me, and much worse, a wrong to the country. My wish is that on this subject no remark be made, nor question asked by any of you, here, or elsewhere, now, or hereafter."

This is one of the most remarkable speeches ever made by a President. Washington was never more dignified; Jackson was never more peremptory.

The President's spirit of forgiveness was broad enough to take in the entire South. The cause of the Confederacy had been doomed from the hour of his reelection. The cheering of the troops which greeted the news had been heard within the lines at Richmond, and the besieged town lost hope, though it continued the struggle bravely if desperately. Although Horace Greeley's peace mission to Canada had come to nothing, and other volunteer efforts in the same direction served only to call forth a declaration from Jefferson Davis that he would fight for the independence of the South to the bitter end, Mr. Lincoln watched longingly for the time when the first move could be made toward peace. Early in January, 1865, as the country was about to enter upon the fifth year of actual war, he learned from Hon. Francis P. Blair, Sr., who had been in Richmond, how strong the feeling of discouragement at the Confederate capital had become. Mr. Blair was the father of Lincoln's first Postmaster-General, a man of large acquaintance in the South, who knew perhaps better than anyone in Washington the character and temper of the southern leaders. He had gone to Richmond hoping to do something toward bringing the war to a close, but without explaining his plans to anyone, and with no authority from the government, beyond permission to pass through the military lines and return. His scheme was utterly impracticable, and Mr. Lincoln was interested in the report of his visit only because it showed that the rebellion was nearing its end. This was so marked that he sent Mr. Blair back again to Richmond with a note intended for the eye of Jefferson Davis, saying that the government had constantly been, was then, and would continue to be ready to receive any agent Mr. Davis might send, "with a view of securing peace to the people of our one common country."

Hopeless as their cause had by this time become, the Confederates had no mind to treat for peace on any terms except independence of the southern States; yet, on the other hand, they were in such straits that they could not afford to leave Mr. Lincoln's offer untested. Mr. Davis therefore sent north his

Vice-President, Alexander H. Stephens, with two other high officials of the Confederate government, armed with instructions which aimed to be liberal enough to gain them admittance to the Union lines, and yet distinctly announced that they came "for the purpose of securing peace to the two countries." This difference in the wording of course doomed their mission in advance, for the government at Washington had never admitted that there were "two countries," and to receive the messengers of Jefferson Davis on any such terms would be to concede practically all that the South asked.

When they reached the Union lines the officer who met them informed them that they could go no farther unless they accepted the President's conditions. They finally changed the form of their request, and were taken to Fortress Monroe. Meantime Mr. Lincoln had sent Secretary Seward to Fortress Monroe with instructions to hear all they might have to say, but not to definitely conclude anything. On learning the true nature of their errand he was about to recall him, when he received a telegram from General Grant, regretting that Mr. Lincoln himself could not see the commissioners, because, to Grant's mind, they seemed sincere.

Anxious to do everything he could in the interest of peace, Mr. Lincoln, instead of recalling Secretary Seward, telegraphed that he would himself come to Fortress Monroe, and started that same night. The next morning, February 3, 1865, he and the Secretary of State received the rebel commissioners on board the President's steamer, the River Queen.

This conference between the two highest officials of the United States government, and three messengers from the Confederacy, bound, as the President well knew beforehand, by instructions which made any practical outcome impossible, brings out, in strongest relief, Mr. Lincoln's kindly patience, even toward the rebellion. He was determined to leave no means untried that might, however remotely, lead to peace. For four hours he patiently answered the many questions they asked him, as to what would probably be done on various subjects if the South submitted; pointing out always the difference between the things that he had the power to decide, and those that must be submitted to Congress; and bringing the discussion back, time and again, to the three points absolutely necessary to secure peace-- Union, freedom for the slaves, and complete disbandment of the Confederate armies. He had gone to offer them, honestly and frankly, the best terms in his power, but not to give up one atom of official dignity or duty. Their main thought, on the contrary, had been to postpone or to escape the express conditions on which they were admitted to the conference.

They returned to Richmond and reported the failure of their efforts to Jefferson Davis, whose disappointment equalled their own, for all had caught eagerly at the hope that this interview would somehow prove a means of escape from the dangers of their situation. President Lincoln, full of kindly thoughts, on the other hand, went back to Washington, intent on making yet one more generous offer to hasten the day of peace. He had told the commissioners that personally he would be in favor of the government paying a liberal amount for the loss of slave property, on condition that the southern States agree of their own accord to the freedom of the slaves.* This was indeed going to the extreme of liberality, but Mr. Lincoln remembered that notwithstanding all their offenses the rebels were American citizens, members of the same nation and brothers of the same blood. He remembered, too, that the object of the war, equally with peace and freedom, was to preserve friendship and to continue the Union. Filled with such thoughts and purposes he spent the day after his return in drawing up a new proposal designed as a peace offering to the States in rebellion. On the evening of February 5 he read this to his cabinet. It offered the southern States $400,000,000 or a sum equal to the cost of war for two hundred days, on condition that all fighting cease by the first of April, 1865. He proved more liberal than any of his advisers; and with the words, "You are all against me," sadly uttered, the President folded up the paper, and ended the discussion.

* Mr. Lincoln had freed the slaves two years before as a military necessity, and as such it had been accepted by all. Yet a question might arise, when the war ended, as to whether this act of his had been lawful. He was therefore very anxious to have freedom find a place in the Constitution of the United States.

This could only be done by an amendment to the Constitution, proposed by Congress, and adopted by the legislatures of three-fourths of the States of the Union. Congress voted in favor of such an amendment on January 31, 1865. Illinois, the President's own State, adopted it on the very next day, and though Mr. Lincoln did not live to see it a part of the Constitution, Secretary Seward, on December 18, 1865, only a few months after Mr. Lincoln's death, was able to make official announcement that 29 States, constituting a majority of three-fourths of the 36 States of the Union, had adopted it, and that therefore it was the law of the land.

Jefferson Davis had issued a last appeal to "fire the southern heart," but the situation at Richmond was becoming desperate Flour cost a thousand dollars a barrel in Confederate money, and neither the flour nor the money were sufficient for their needs. Squads of guards were sent into the streets with directions to arrest every able-bodied man they met, and force him to work in defense of the town. It is said that the medical boards were ordered to excuse no one from military service who was well enough to bear arms for even ten days. Human nature will not endure a strain like this, and desertion grew too common to punish. Nevertheless the city kept up its defense until April 3. Even then, although hopelessly beaten, the Confederacy was not willing to give in, and much needless and severe fighting took place before the final end came. The rebel government hurried away toward the South, and Lee bent all his energies to saving his army and taking it to join General Johnston, who still held out against Sherman. Grant pursued him with such energy that he did not even allow himself the pleasure of entering the captured rebel capital. The chase continued six days. On the evening of April 8 the Union army succeeded in planting itself squarely across Lee's line of retreat; and the marching and fighting of his army were over for ever. On the next morning the two generals met in a house on the edge of the village of Appomattox, Virginia, Lee resplendent in a new uniform and handsome sword, Grant in the travel-stained garments in which he had made the campaign--the blouse of a private soldier, with the shoulderstraps of a Lieutenant-General. Here the surrender took place. Grant, as courteous in victory as he was energetic in war, offered Lee terms that were liberal in the extreme; and on learning that the Confederate soldiers were actually suffering with hunger, ordered that rations be issued to them at once.

Fire and destruction attended the flight of the Confederates from Richmond. Jefferson Davis and his cabinet, carrying with them their more important state papers, left the doomed city on one of the crowded and overloaded railroad trains on the night of April 2, beginning a southward flight that ended only with Mr. Davis's capture about a month later. The legislature of Virginia and the governor of the State departed hurriedly on a canal-boat in the direction of Lynchburg, while every possible carriage or vehicle was pressed into service by the inhabitants, all frantic to get away before their city was "desecrated" by the presence of the Yankees. By the time the military left, early on the morning of April 3, the town was on fire. The Confederate Congress had ordered all government tobacco and other public property to be burned. The rebel General Ewell, who was in charge of the city, asserts that he took the responsibility of disobeying, and that the fires were not started by his orders. Be that as it may, they broke out in various places, while a mob, crazed with excitement, and wild with the alcohol that had run freely in the gutters the night before, rushed from store to store, breaking in the doors, and indulging in all the wantonness of pillage and greed. Public spirit seemed paralyzed; no real effort was made to put out the flames, and as a final horror, the convicts from the penitentiary, overpowering their guards, appeared upon the streets, a maddened, shouting, leaping crowd, drunk with liberty.

It is quite possible that the very size and suddenness of the disaster served in a measure to lessen its evil effects; for the burning of seven hundred buildings, the entire business portion of Richmond, all in the brief space of a day, was a visitation so sudden, so stupefying and unexpected as to overawe and terrorize even evildoers. Before a new danger could arise help was at hand. Gen. Weitzel, to whom the city surrendered, took up his headquarters in the house lately occupied by Jefferson Davis, and promptly set about the work of relief; fighting the fire, issuing rations to the poor, and restoring order and authority. That a regiment of black soldiers assisted in this work of mercy must have seemed to the white inhabitants of Richmond the final drop in their cup of misery.

Into the rebel capital, thus stricken and laid waste, came President Lincoln on the morning of April 4. Never in the history of the world has the head of a mighty nation and the conqueror of a great rebellion entered the captured chief city of the insurgents in such humbleness and simplicity. He had gone two weeks before to City Point for a visit to General Grant, and to his son, Captain Robert Lincoln, who was serving on Grant's staff. Making his home on the steamer that brought him, and enjoying what was probably the most restful and satisfactory holiday in which he had been able to indulge during his whole presidential service, he had visited the various camps of the great army, in company with the General, cheered everywhere by the loving greetings of the soldiers. He had met Sherman when that commander hurried up fresh from his victorious march from Atlanta; and after Grant had started on his final pursuit of Lee the President still lingered. It was at City Point that the news came to him of the fall of Richmond.

Between the receipt of this news and the following forenoon, before any information of the great fire had reached them, a visit to the rebel capital was arranged for the President and Rear Admiral Porter. Ample precautions for their safety were taken at the start. The President went in his own steamer, the River Queen, with her escort, the Bat, and a tug used at City Point in landing from the steamer. Admiral Porter went in his flagship; while a transport carried a small cavalry escort, as well as ambulances for the party. Barriers in the river soon made it impossible to proceed in this fashion, and one unforeseen accident after another rendered it necessary to leave behind the larger and even the smaller boats; until finally the party went on in the Admiral's barge rowed by twelve sailors, without escort of any kind. In this manner the President made his entry into Richmond, landing near Libby Prison. As the party stepped ashore they found a guide among the contrabands who quickly crowded the streets, for the possible coming of the President had already been noised through the city. Ten of the sailors armed with carbines were formed as a guard, six in front, and four in rear, and between them the President and Admiral Porter, with the three officers who accompanied them, walked the long distance, perhaps a mile and a half, to the centre of the town.

Imagination can easily fill in the picture of a gradually increasing crowd, principally of negroes, following the little group of marines and officers with the tall form of the President in its centre; and, when they learned that it was indeed "Massa Lincum," expressing their joy and gratitude in fervent blessings and in the deep emotional cries of the colored race. It is easy also to imagine the sharp anxiety of those who had the President's safety in their charge during this tiresome and even foolhardy march through a town still in flames, whose white inhabitants were sullenly resentful at best, and whose grief and anger might at any moment break out against the man they looked upon as the chief author of their misfortunes. No accident befell him. He reached General Weitzel's headquarters in safety, rested in the house Jefferson Davis had occupied while President of the Confederacy; and after a day of sightseeing returned to his steamer and to Washington, there to be stricken down by an assassin's bullet, literally "in the house of his friends."

XIII. THE FOURTEENTH OF APRIL

Refreshed in body by his visit to City Point and greatly cheered by the fall of Richmond, and unmistakable signs that the war was over, Mr. Lincoln went back to Washington intent on the new task opening before him--that of restoring the Union, and of bringing about peace and good will again between the North and the South. His whole heart was bent on the work of "binding up the nation's wounds" and doing all which lay in his power to "achieve a just and lasting peace." Especially did he desire to avoid the shedding of blood, or anything like acts of deliberate punishment. He talked to his cabinet in this strain on the morning of April 14, the last day of his life. "No one need expect that he would take any part in hanging or killing these men, even the worst of them," he exclaimed. Enough lives had been sacrificed already. Anger must be put aside. The great need now was to begin to act in the interest of peace. With these words of clemency and kindness in their ears they left him, never again to come together under his wise chairmanship.

Though it was invariably held in check by his vigorous common-sense, there was in Mr. Lincoln's nature a strong vein of poetry and mysticism. That morning he told his cabinet a strange story of a dream that he had had the night before--a dream which he said came to him before great events. He had dreamed it before the battles of Antietam, Murfreesboro, Gettysburg and Vicksburg. This time it must foretell a victory by Sherman over Johnston's army, news of which was hourly expected, for he knew of no other important event likely to occur. The members of the cabinet were deeply impressed; but General Grant, who had come to Washington that morning and was present, remarked with matter-of-fact exactness that Murfreesboro was no victory and had no important results. Not the wildest imagination of skeptic or mystic could have pictured the events under which the day was to close.

It was Good Friday, a day observed by a portion of the people with fasting and prayer, but even among the most devout the great news of the week just ended changed this time of traditional mourning into a season of general thanksgiving. For Mr. Lincoln it was a day of unusual and quiet happiness. His son Robert had returned from the field with General Grant, and the President spent an hour with the young captain in delighted conversation over the campaign. He denied himself generally to visitors, admitting only a few friends. In the afternoon he went for a long drive with Mrs. Lincoln. His mood, as it had been all day, was singularly happy and tender. He talked much of the past and future. After four years of trouble and tumult he looked forward to four years of quiet and normal work; after that he expected to go back again to Illinois and practice law. He was never more simple or more gentle than on this day of triumph. His heart overflowed with sentiments of gratitude to Heaven, which took the shape, usual to generous natures, of love and kindness to all men.

From the very beginning there had been threats to kill him. He was constantly receiving letters of warning from zealous or nervous friends. The War Department inquired into these when there seemed to be ground for doing so, but always without result. Warnings that appeared most definite proved on examination too vague and confused for further attention. The President knew that he was in some danger. Madmen frequently made their way to the very door of the Executive Office; sometimes into Mr. Lincoln's presence; but he himself had so sane a mind, and a heart so kindly even to his enemies, that it was hard for him to believe in political hatred deadly enough to lead to murder. He summed up the matter by saying that since he must receive both friends and strangers every day, his life was of course within the reach of any one, sane or mad, who was ready to murder and be hanged for it, and that he could not possibly guard against all danger unless he shut himself up in an iron box, where he could scarcely perform the duties of a President.

He therefore went in and out before the people, always unarmed, generally unattended. He received hundreds of visitors in a day, his breast bare to pistol or knife. He walked at midnight, with a single Secretary or alone, from the Executive Mansion to the War Department and back. In summer he rode through lonely roads from the White House to the Soldiers' Home in the dusk of the evening, and returned to his work in the morning before the town was astir. He was greatly annoyed when it was decided that there must be a guard at the Executive Mansion, and that a squad of cavalry must accompany him on his daily drive; but he was always reasonable, and yielded to the best judgment of others.

Four years of threats and boastings that were unfounded, and of plots that came to nothing passed away, until precisely at the time when the triumph of the nation seemed assured, and a feeling of peace and security settled over the country, one of the conspiracies, seemingly no more important than the others, ripened in a sudden heat of hatred and despair.

A little band of desperate secessionists, of which John Wilkes Booth, an actor of a family of famous players, was the head, had their usual meeting-place at the house of Mrs. Mary E. Surratt, the mother of one of the number. Booth was a young man of twenty-six, strikingly handsome, with an ease and grace of manner which came to him of right from his theatrical ancestors. He was a fanatical southerner, with a furious hatred against Lincoln and the Union. After Lincoln's reelection he went to Canada, and associated with the

Confederate agents there; and whether or not with their advice, made a plan to capture the President and take him to Richmond. He passed a great part of the autumn and winter pursuing this fantastic scheme, but the winter wore away, and nothing was done. On March 4 he was at the Capitol, and created a disturbance by trying to force his way through the line of policemen who guarded the passage through which the President walked to the East front of the building to read his Second Inaugural. His intentions at this time are not known. He afterwards said he lost an excellent chance of killing the President that day.

After the surrender of Lee, in a rage akin to madness, he called his fellow-conspirators together and allotted to each his part in the new crime which had risen in his mind. It was as simple as it was horrible. One man was to kill Secretary Seward, another to make way with Andrew Johnson, at the same time that he murdered the President. The final preparations were made with feverish haste. It was only about noon of the fourteenth that Booth learned that Mr. Lincoln meant to go to Ford's Theatre that night to see the play "Our American Cousin." The President enjoyed the theatre. It was one of his few means of recreation, and as the town was then thronged with soldiers and officers all eager to see him, he could, by appearing in public, gratify many whom he could not personally meet.

Mrs. Lincoln asked General and Mrs. Grant to accompany her. They accepted, and the announcement that they would be present was made in the evening papers, but they changed their plans and went north by an afternoon train. Mrs. Lincoln then invited in their stead Miss Harris and Major Rathbone, daughter and stepson of Senator Ira Harris. Being detained by visitors, the play had made some progress when the President appeared.. The band struck up "Hail to the Chief," the actors ceased playing, the audience rose and cheered, the President bowed in acknowledgment, and the play went on again.

From the moment he learned of the President's intention Booth's actions were alert and energetic. He and his confederates were seen in every part of the city. Booth was perfectly at home in Ford's Theatre. He counted upon audacity to reach the small passage behind the President's box. Once there, he guarded against interference by arranging a wooden bar, to be fastened by a simple mortice in the angle of the wall and the door by which he entered, so that once shut, the door could not be opened from the outside. He even provided for the chance of not gaining entrance to the box by boring a hole in the door, through which he might either observe the occupants, or take aim and shoot. He hired at a livery stable a small fleet horse.

A few moments before ten o'clock, leaving his horse at the rear of the theatre, in charge of a call-boy, he entered the building, passing rapidly to the little hallway leading to the President's box. Showing a card to the servant in attendance, he was allowed to enter, closed the door noiselessly, and secured it with the wooden bar he had made ready, without disturbing any of the occupants of the box, between whom and himself yet remained the partition and the door through which he had bored the hole.

No one, not even the actor who uttered them, could ever remember the last words of the piece that were spoken that night--the last that Abraham Lincoln heard upon earth; for the tragedy in the box turned play and players alike to the most unsubstantial of phantoms. For weeks hate and brandy had kept Booth's brain in a morbid state. He seemed to himself to be taking part in a great play. Holding a pistol in one hand and a knife in the other, he opened the box door, put the pistol to the President's head, and fired. Major Rathbone sprang to grapple with him, and received a savage knife wound in the arm. Then, rushing forward, Booth placed his hand on the railing of the box and vaulted to the stage. It was a high leap, but nothing to such a trained athlete. He would have got safely away, had not his spur caught in the flag that draped the front of the box. He fell, the torn flag trailing on his spur; but though the fall had broken his leg, he rose instantly brandishing his knife and shouting, "Sic Semper Tyrannis!" fled rapidly across the stage and out of sight. Major Rathbone shouted, "Stop him!" The cry, "He has shot the President!" rang through the theatre, and from the audience, stupid at first with surprise, and wild afterward with excitement and horror, men jumped upon the stage in pursuit of the assassin. But he ran through the familiar passages, leaped upon his horse, rewarding with a kick and a curse the boy who held him, and escaped into the night.

The President scarcely moved. His head drooped forward slightly, his eyes closed. Major Rathbone, not regarding his own grievous hurt, rushed to the door to summon aid. He found it barred, and someone on the outside beating and clamoring to get in. It was at once seen that the President's wound was mortal. He was carried across the street to a house opposite, and laid upon a bed. Mrs. Lincoln followed, tenderly cared for by Miss Harris. Rathbone, exhausted by loss of blood, fainted, and was taken home. Messengers were sent for the cabinet, for the Surgeon-General, for Dr. Stone the President's family physician, and for others whose official or private relations with Mr. Lincoln gave them the right to be there. A crowd of people rushed instinctively to the White House, and bursting through the doors shouted the dreadful news to Robert Lincoln and Major Hay who sat together in an upper room.

The President had been shot a few minutes after ten o'clock. The wound would have brought instant death to most men. He was unconscious from the first moment, but he breathed throughout the night, his gaunt face scarcely paler than those of the sorrowing men around him. At twenty-two minutes past seven in the morning he died. Secretary Stanton broke the silence by saying, "Now he belongs to the ages."

Booth had done his work thoroughly. His principal accomplice had acted with equal audacity and cruelty, but with less fatal result. Under pretext of having a package of medicine to deliver, he forced his way to the room of the Secretary of State, who lay ill, and attacked him, inflicting three terrible knife wounds on his neck and cheek, wounding also the Secretary's two sons, a servant, and a soldier nurse who tried to overpower him. Finally breaking away, he ran downstairs, reached the door unhurt, and springing upon his horse rode off. It was feared that neither the Secretary nor his eldest son would live, but both in time recovered.

Although Booth had been recognized by dozens of people as he stood before the footlights brandishing his dagger, his swift horse soon carried him beyond any hap-hazard pursuit. He crossed the Navy Yard bridge and rode into Maryland, being joined by one of his fellow-conspirators. A surgeon named Mudd set Booth's leg and sent him on his desolate way. For ten days the two men lived the lives of hunted animals. On the night of April 25 they were surrounded as they lay sleeping in a barn in Caroline County, Virginia. Booth refused to surrender. The barn was fired, and while it was burning he was shot by Boston Corbett, a sergeant of cavalry. He lingered for about three hours in great pain, and died at seven in the morning. The remaining conspirators were tried by military commission. Four were hanged, including the assailant of Secretary Seward, and the others were sentenced to imprisonment for various lengths of time.

Upon the hearts of a people glowing with the joy of victory the news of the President's death fell as a great shock. In the unspeakable calamity the country lost sight of the great national successes of the past week; and thus it came to pass that there was never any organized celebration in the North over the downfall of the rebellion. It was unquestionably best that it should be so. Lincoln himself would not have had it otherwise, for he hated the arrogance of triumph. As it was, the South could take no offense at a grief so genuine; and the people of that section even shared, to a certain extent, in the mourning for one who, in their inmost hearts, they knew to have wished them well.

Within an hour after Mr. Lincoln's body was taken to the White House the town was shrouded in black. Not only the public buildings, the shops, and the better class of dwellings were draped in funeral decorations; still more touching proof of affection was shown in the poorest class of homes, where laboring men of both colors found means in their poverty to afford some scanty bit of mourning. The interest and veneration of the people still centered at the White House, where, under a tall catafalque in the East Room the late chief lay in the majesty of death, rather than in the modest tavern on Pennsylvania Avenue, where the new President had his lodgings, and where the Chief Justice administered the oath of office to him at eleven o'clock on the morning of April 15.

It was determined that the funeral ceremonies in Washington should be held on Wednesday, April 19, and all the churches throughout the country were invited to join at the same time in appropriate observances. The ceremonies in the East Room were simple and brief, while all the pomp and circumstance that the government could command were employed to give a fitting escort from the Executive Mansion to the Capitol, where the body of the President lay in state. The procession moved to the booming of minute guns, and the tolling of all the bells in Washington, Georgetown and Alexandria; while, to associate the pomp of the day with the greatest work of Lincoln's life, a detachment of colored troops marched at the head of the line.

When it was announced that he was to be buried at Springfield every town and city on the way begged that the train might halt within its limits, to give its people opportunity of showing their grief and reverence. It was finally arranged that the funeral cortege should follow substantially the same route over which Lincoln had come in 1861 to take possession of the office to which he added a new dignity and value for all time. On April 21, accompanied by a guard of honor, and in a train decked with somber trappings, the journey was begun. At Baltimore, through which, four years before, it was a question whether the President-elect could pass with safety to his life, the coffin was taken with reverent care to the great dome of the Exchange, where, surrounded with evergreens and lilies, it lay for several hours, the people passing by in mournful throngs. The same demonstration was repeated, gaining constantly in depth of feeling and solemn splendor of display in every city through which the procession passed. In New York came General Scott, pale and feeble, but resolute, to pay his tribute of respect to his departed friend and commander.

Springfield was reached on the morning of May 3. The body lay in state in the Capitol, which was richly draped from roof to basement in black velvet and silver fringe, while within it was a bower of bloom and fragrance. For twenty-four hours an unbroken stream of people passed through, bidding their friend and neighbor welcome home and farewell. At ten o'clock on the morning of May 4 the coffin lid was closed, and vast procession moved out to

Oak Ridge, where the town had set apart a lovely spot for his grave. Here the dead President was committed to the soil of the State which had so loved and honored him. The ceremonies at the grave were simple and touching. Bishop Simpson delivered a pathetic oration, prayers were offered, and hymns were sung, but the weightiest and most eloquent words uttered anywhere that day were those of the Second Inaugural, which the Committee had wisely ordained to be read over his grave, as centuries before, the friends of the painter Raphael chose the incomparable canvas of "The Transfiguration" to be the chief ornament of his funeral.

Though President Lincoln lived to see the real end of the war, various bodies of Confederate troops continued to hold out for some time longer. General Johnston faced Sherman's army in the Carolinas until April 26, while General E. Kirby Smith, west of the Mississippi River, did not surrender until May 26.

As rapidly as possible Union volunteer regiments were disbanded, and soon the mighty host of 1,000,000 men was reduced to a peace footing of only 25,000. Before the great army melted away into the greater body of citizens its soldiers enjoyed one final triumph--a march through the capital of the nation, undisturbed by death or danger, under the eyes of their highest commanders and the representatives of the people whose country they had saved. Those who witnessed the solemn yet joyous pageant will never forget it; and pray that their children may never see its like. For two days this formidable host marched the long stretch of Pennsylvania Avenue, starting from the shadow of the Capitol and filling the wide street as far as Georgetown, its serried ranks moving with the easy yet rapid pace of veterans in cadence step. As a mere spectacle this march of the mightiest host the continent has ever seen was grand and imposing, but it was not as a spectacle alone that it affected the beholder. It was no holiday parade. It was an army of citizens on their way home after a long and terrible war. Their clothes were worn, and pierced with bullets, their banners had been torn with shot and shell, and lashed in the winds of many battles. The very drums and fifes had called out the troops to night alarms, and sounded the onset on historic fields. The whole country claimed these heroes as part of themselves. They were not soldiers by profession or from love of fighting; they had become soldiers only to save their country's life. Now, done with war, they were going joyously and peaceably back to their homes to take up the tasks they had willingly laid down in the hour of their country's need.

Friends loaded them with flowers as they swung down the Avenue-- both men and officers, until some were fairly hidden under their fragrant burden. Grotesque figures were not absent, as Sherman's legions passed with their "bummers" and their regimental pets. But with all the shouting and the joy there was, in the minds of all who saw it, one sad and ever-recurring thought-- the memory of the men who were absent, and who had, nevertheless, so richly earned the right to be there. The soldiers in their shrunken companies thought of the brave comrades who had fallen by the way; and through the whole vast army there was passionate unavailing regret for their wise, gentle and powerful friend Abraham Lincoln, gone forever from the big white house by the Avenue--who had called the great host into being, directed the course of the nation during the four years that they had been battling for its life, and to whom, more than to any other, this crowning peaceful pageant would have been full of deep and happy meaning.

Why was this man so loved that his death caused a whole nation to forget its triumph, and turned its gladness into mourning? Why has his fame grown with the passing years until now scarcely a speech is made or a newspaper printed that does not have within it somewhere a mention of his name or some phrase or sentence that fell from his lips? Let us see if we can, what it was that made Abraham Lincoln the man that he became.

A child born to an inheritance of want; a boy growing into a narrow world of ignorance; a youth taking up the burden of coarse and heavy labor; a man entering on the doubtful struggle of a local backwoods career--these were the beginnings of Abraham Lincoln if we look at them only in the hard practical spirit which takes for its motto that "Nothing succeeds but success. If we adopt a more generous as well as a truer view, then we see that it was the brave hopeful spirit, the strong active mind, and the great law of moral growth that accepts the good and rejects the bad, which Nature gave this obscure child, that carried him to the service of mankind and the admiration of the centuries as certainly as the acorn grows to be the oak.

Even his privations helped the end. Self-reliance, the strongest trait of the pioneer was his by blood and birth and training, and was developed by the hardships of his lot to the mighty power needed to guide our country through the struggle of the Civil War.

The sense of equality was his also, for he grew from childhood to manhood in a state of society where there were neither rich to envy nor poor to despise, and where the gifts and hardships of the forest were distributed without favor to each and all alike. In the forest he learned charity, sympathy, helpfulness--in a word neighborliness--for in that far-off frontier life all the wealth of India, had a man possessed it, could not have bought relief from danger or help in time of need, and neighborliness became of prime importance. Constant opportunity was found there to practice the virtue which Christ declared to be next to the love of God--to love one's neighbor as oneself.

In such settlements, far removed from courts and jails, men were brought face to face with questions of natural right. The pioneers not only understood the American doctrine of self-government--they lived it. It was this understanding, this feeling, which taught Lincoln to write: "When the white man governs himself, that is self-government; but when he governs himself and also governs another man, that is more than self-government that is despotism;" and also to give utterance to its twin truth: "He who would be no slave must consent to have no slave."

Lincoln was born in the slave State of Kentucky. He lived there only a short time, and we have reason to believe that wherever he might have grown up, his very nature would have spurned the doctrine and practice of human slavery. Yet, though he hated slavery, he never hated the slave-holder. His feeling of pardon and sympathy for Kentucky and the South played no unimportant part in his dealings with grave problems of statesmanship. It is true that he struck slavery its death blow with the hand of war, but at the same time he offered the slaveowner golden payment with the hand of peace.

Abraham Lincoln was not an ordinary man. He was, in truth, in the language of the poet Lowell, a "new birth of our new soil." His greatness did not consist in growing up on the frontier. An ordinary man would have found on the frontier exactly what he would have found elsewhere--a commonplace life, varying only with the changing ideas and customs of time and place. But for the man with extraordinary powers of mind and body--for one gifted by Nature as Abraham Lincoln was gifted, the pioneer life with its severe training in self-denial, patience and industry, developed his character, and fitted him for the great duties of his after life as no other training could have done.

His advancement in the astonishing career that carried him from obscurity to world-wide fame--from postmaster of New Salem village to President of the United States, from captain of a backwoods volunteer company to Commander-in-Chief of the Army and Navy, was neither sudden nor accidental, nor easy. He was both ambitious and successful, but his ambition was moderate, and his success was slow. And, because his success was slow, it never outgrew either his judgment or his powers. Between the day when he left his father's cabin and launched his canoe on the headwaters of the Sangamon River to begin life on his own account, and the day of his first inauguration, lay full thirty years of toil, self-denial, patience; often of effort baffled, of hope deferred; sometimes of bitter disappointment. Even with the natural gift of great genius it required an average lifetime and faithful unrelaxing effort, to transform the raw country stripling into a fit ruler for this great nation.

Almost every success was balanced--sometimes overbalanced, by a seeming failure. He went into the Black Hawk war a captain, and through no fault of his own, came out a private. He rode to the hostile frontier on horseback, and trudged home on foot. His store "winked out." His surveyor's compass and chain, with which he was earning a scanty living, were sold for debt. He was defeated in his first attempts to be nominated for the legislature and for

Congress; defeated in his application to be appointed Commissioner of the General Land Office; defeated for the Senate when he had forty-five votes to begin with. by a man who had only five votes to begin with; defeated again after his joint debates with Douglas; defeated in the nomination for Vice-President, when a favorable nod from half a dozen politicians would have brought him success.

Failures? Not so. Every seeming defeat was a slow success. His was the growth of the oak, and not of Jonah's gourd. He could not become a master workman until he had served a tedious apprenticeship. It was the quarter of a century of reading, thinking, speech-making and lawmaking which fitted him to be the chosen champion of freedom in the great Lincoln-Douglas debates of 1858. It was the great moral victory won in those debates (although the senatorship went to Douglas) added to the title "Honest Old Abe," won by truth and manhood among his neighbors during a whole lifetime, that led the people of the United States to trust him with the duties and powers of President.

And when, at last, after thirty years of endeavor, success had beaten down defeat, when Lincoln had been nominated, elected and inaugurated, came the crowning trial of his faith and constancy. When the people, by free and lawful choice, had placed honor and power in his hands, when his name could convene Congress, approve laws, cause ships to sail and armies to move, there suddenly came upon the government and the nation a fatal paralysis. Honor seemed to dwindle and power to vanish. Was he then after all not to be President? Was patriotism dead? Was the Constitution only a bit of waste paper? Was the Union gone?

The outlook was indeed grave. There was treason in Congress, treason in the Supreme Court, treason in the army and navy. Confusion and discord were everywhere. To use Mr. Lincoln's forcible figure of speech, sinners were calling the righteous to repentance. Finally the flag, insulted and fired upon, trailed in surrender at Sumter; and then came the humiliation of the riot at Baltimore, and the President for a few days practically a prisoner in the capital of the nation.

But his apprenticeship had been served, and there was to be no more failure. With faith and justice and generosity he conducted for four long years a war whose frontiers stretched from the Potomac to the Rio Grande; whose soldiers numbered a million men on each side. The labor, the thought, the responsibility, the strain of mind and anguish of soul that he gave to this great task, who can measure? "Here was place for no holiday magistrate, no fair weather sailor," as Emerson justly said of him. "The new pilot was hurried to the helm in a tornado. In four years-- four years of battle days--his endurance, his fertility of resources, his magnanimity, were sorely tried and never found wanting." "By his courage, his justice, his even temper, his humanity, he stood a heroic figure in the centre of a heroic epoch."

What but a lifetime's schooling in disappointment, what but the pioneer's self-reliance and freedom from prejudice, what but the clear mind, quick to see natural right and unswerving in its purpose to follow it; what but the steady self-control, the unwarped sympathy, the unbounded charity of this man with spirit so humble and soul so great, could have carried him through the labors he wrought to the victory he attained?

With truth it could be written, "His heart was as great as the world, but there was no room in it to hold the memory of a wrong." So, "with malice toward none, with charity for all, with firmness in the right as God gave him to see the right" he lived and died. We who have never seen him yet feel daily the influence of his kindly life, and cherish among our most precious possessions the heritage of his example.

###

Made in the USA
Middletown, DE
20 September 2023

38833780R00080